WORKING LIVES

Nursing

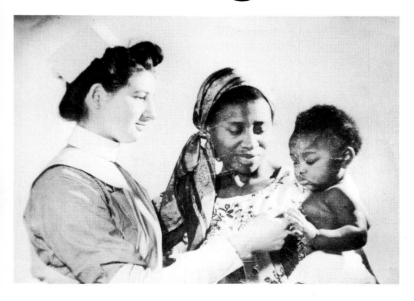

Pat Hodgson

B T BATSFORD LTD   LONDON

Typeset by Tek-Art Ltd, Kent
and printed in Great Britain by
R.J. Acford
Chichester, Sussex
for the publishers
B.T. Batsford Ltd
4 Fitzhardinge Street
London W1H 0AH

ISBN 0 7134 5021 5

Frontispiece
*Mary Ireland at St John's & St Elizabeth's Hospital
during the Second World War*

Cover illustrations
*The colour photograph shows the Special Care Baby
Unit at the Charing Cross Hospital (Charing Cross
Hospital); the black and white illustration is a sixteenth-
century engraving of a ward in Hôtel-Dieu, Paris (Pat
Hodgson Library); the portrait is of a nurse in 1910
(Batsford Archives).*

Acknowledgments
The Author and Publishers would like to thank the
following for their kind permission to use copyright
illustrations: BBC Hulton Picture Library for figures 19,
22, 23, 24, 27, 28, 30, 31, 32, 36, 40 and 49; Cape Warwick
Ltd for figure 42; Charing Cross Hospital for figures 8,
26 and 43; Marie Curie Foundation for figure 46;
Department of Health and Social Security for figures 1,
2 and 34; English National Board of Health Visitors for
figure 47; GLC for figures 9, 25 and 33; Audrey Gray for
figure 48; Pat Hodgson Library for figures 3, 4, 7, 16, 41,
45 and 50; Imperial War Museum for figures 12, 13, 14,
17 and 18; Mary Ireland for the frontispiece and figure
29; Florine Irwin for figure 11; The Archivist, Middlesex
Hospital for figures 7 and 35; National Army Museum
for figures 5 and 10; Michael Russell (Publishing) Ltd
for figure 15; St Mary's Hospital for figure 44; Topham
for figures 37, 38 and 39; Constance Wyatt for figures 20
and 21.

The Author would like to give her special thanks to all
the nurses past and present who contributed their
memories to this book.

Contents

List of Illustrations

Introduction

On 7 June 1860 an advertisement appeared in *The Times* asking for trainees to join Florence Nightingale's new School of Nursing at St Thomas's Hospital, London. The advertisers promised a year's training for suitable women:

... between 25 and 35 years of age, for whom they will provide, free of expense, board and lodging in the Hospital, with tea, sugar, and washing, and a certain amount of outer clothing. A payment will be allowed them of £10 for the year. They will be under the charge of the Matron, and will be instructed by the Sisters and the Resident Medical Officer. At the end of the year, if their training has been found satisfactory, their names will be entered in the Committee's register, and they will be recommended for situations as hospital nurses.

Florence Nightingale hoped that her advertisement would attract girls from the servant class, but soon realized that her future leaders would more likely be found among the better-educated. To attract these girls, from 1865 another tier was recruited. 'Special Probationers' would be drawn from the better-educated professional classes, and paid for their year's training. They were expected to have 'a settled purpose to do the work, free from all romance and affectation' and be 'possessed of that valuable and uncommon quality common sense'. (GLC H1/ST/N7S/C30a) 'Ordinary Probationers' would receive two years' training and have enough education to be able to report on patients, as well as carry out 'the Doctor's and Sister's orders

1 *Nursing recruitment in the 1950s. The shadow of Florence Nightingale is in the background.*

TRAIN TO BE A

NURSE

...a **distinguished career**

There's no career more interesting or worthwhile than the nurse's. Nearly everyone at some time depends on a nurse: nurses are among the most respected and admired members of the community.

You are paid during training. Uniform is free. There are training hospitals throughout the country. You will make many friends if you decide to be a nurse.

For further details apply to :—

implicitly'. They would have as much chance of promotion as the 'Special Probationers'.

Soon, other training colleges opened on the Nightingale model and Nightingale nurses advised on care in Poor Law infirmaries, where the old and chronically sick poor were nursed by untrained fellow paupers. In spite of Florence Nightingale's hopes, insufficient 'Special Probationers' applied for training until war broke out in 1914, when it was considered patriotic to become a nurse. During the 1920s and 1930s numbers fell again, partly because the one-tier state registration exam, which started in 1919, put off girls without much schooling. Pay was also low. Advertising for staff in 1934, the Radcliffe Infirmary said that recruits should be between 19 and 30 and 'well educated'. They would have three years' training and a salary of between £20 and £30 a year. A matron at the Minehead and West Somerset Hospital was offered a starting salary of £170 the same year.

A vigorous recruitment campaign for nurses started after the National Health Service was formed in 1948. As a result of the Second World War married women were now accepted by the profession and men were also encouraged to join. Recruitment literature in 1958 promised the latter 'Good Pay, Good Prospects, and Deferred "Call Up" '. An additional grade of State Enrolled Nurse had been created in 1943, having a shorter, more practical training than the State Registered Nurse. In 1956 the average training salary was between £260 and £285 a year, for a 96-hour fortnight, four weeks' leave and a full day off each week.

Today's recruiting posters look very different from those of the 1950s. Instead of showing a pretty nurse carrying a tray, they illustrate new technology in medicine and the nurse's part in it. The emphasis is on professionalism and specialization. Nurses work a 37½ hour-week, with two days off and are entitled to a minimum of four weeks' holiday. At the time of writing, salaries for student nurses range from £3917 to £4277 per year. Academic qualifications are becoming more important. Nowadays, candidates for nursing need at least 5 'O' Levels. Nurses can take degrees and doctorates. A nurse in management at the top of the profession can reach a salary of £26,000 (April 1985).

The nursing profession has travelled far in a hundred years. In the course of this book we will hear from nurses themselves what it was like to work as a nurse in the past and what it is like today.

---

2 *This 1980s advertisement emphasizes the professional status of nursing.*

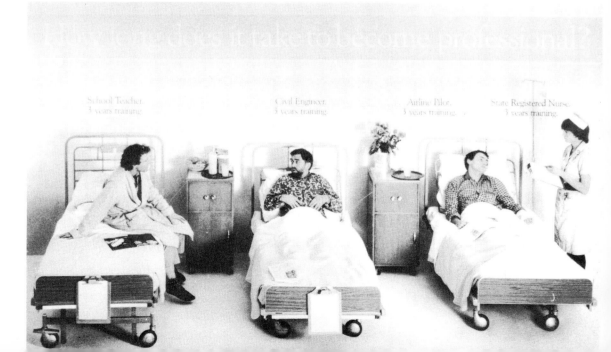

1 The Start of Trained Nursing

Nursing before 1859

Although it is common to think that nursing started with Florence Nightingale, there were, of course, plenty of nurses before her. In earlier times, nursing was carried out at home, mainly by relatives; hospitals were only used by the poor and chronically ill. By the nineteenth century, nurses, apart from a patient's family, fell into four categories, each with little formal training. First there were nursing sisters in religious orders. Next came pauper nurses, who looked after their fellow inmates in workhouses. Thirdly there were the servant/nurses in voluntary hospitals. The last category, midwives, had already made attempts to become an independent profession, and since the eighteenth century formal training could be obtained at Lying-In hospitals.

Charles Dickens had not helped the nursing profession's reputation when he invented the character of Sarah Gamp, in his book *Martin Chuzzlewit* (1848). After gulping down a 'shilling's worth of gin', Sarah gave the patient his medicine 'by the simple process of clutching his windpipe, to make him gasp, and immediately pouring it down his throat'. The accusation of drunkenness, however, may have had some foundation, as alcohol was cheap and was even given in part wages to nurses at some hospitals at that time.

3 *A nun from a French nursing order in the eighteenth century. The first nurses' uniforms were partly derived from those worn by nursing nuns.*

Male and female roles in medicine

Although Florence Nightingale's reforms were based on a clear distinction between male doctors and female nurses/midwives, this had not always been the case. Throughout history it was women who had dealt with healing, child-birth, sickness and death within their own households, sometimes also treating their neighbours. They prescribed herbal medicines and were often the only healers that ordinary people consulted, as doctors were few and far between until the eighteenth century. The Reverent Colfe of Lewisham inscribed on his wife's tomb in 1643 that she had been for 40 years 'a willing nurse, midwife, surgeon and, in part, physician, to all, both rich and poor, without expecting reward'. On the other hand, male midwives became the fashion for a time during the seventeenth and eighteenth centuries, and there had always been male nurses to look after asylum inmates – although they were more like prison warders than nurses until the asylum reforms of the nineteenth century.

4 *Ward at St Bartholomew's Hospital in 1833. The beds are wooden and have heavy, unhygienic curtains round them.*

Voluntary hospitals in the early nineteenth century

The hospitals in which the pre-Nightingale nurses worked were either supported by charity (voluntary hospitals) or were Poor Law infirmaries (workhouses). Writing in 1857, a St Thomas's surgeon said that voluntary hospital nurses were 'of the level of housemaids and required little teaching beyond poultice-making, bed-making and hygiene' (Alan Delgado, *A Hundred Years of Medical Care*). When a new nurse was needed a servant was generally promoted rather than advertising. Hospitals were dusty, insanitary places where the sick lay on clumsy wooden beds, shrouded by curtains, which were a breeding ground for 'spiders, mice nests and bedbugs', according to one nineteenth-century doctor. Nurses worked very long hours. Two visitors to the London Hospital in the 1840s reported that they had seen nurses 'overcome by sleep while on their duty, and the health of many

5 *Florence Nightingale on night duty at Scutari during the Crimean War, with 'lamp in hand'*

of them has given way under their arduous labours.' (A.E. Clark-Kennedy, *The London*, Vol 2.) Pay at this period was between 6s. and 9s. 6d. a week, plus beer and food in some cases. Nurses slept off the wards in rooms which Florence Nightingale described as 'wooden cages on the landing places' or in 'damp and ill ventilated rooms in the basement' (quoted in Brian Abel-Smith, *A History of the Nursing Profession*).

Poor Law infirmaries

Pauper nurses were rated at the bottom of the nursing scale. Workhouse reformer Louisa Twining wrote in 1866:

'To be the lowest scrubber in any hospital is estimated a higher post than to be nurse with the sole charge of a workhouse ward and none will fill it who can live elsewhere. (Quoted in *A History of the Nursing Profession*)

Many pauper nurses were illiterate, elderly or frail and few left accounts of their lives. One, however, does give a glimpse of conditions at the Strand Union in the mid-nineteenth century. Her room was:

on the same Floor as the Men's Sick Ward; only a small Lobby parted us. In this Lobby was a Sink and a Dusthole; there also was all the soiled Linen . . . . I often got the smell so strong from the same in my Room that I could scarcely bear to remain in it. (J. Rogers, *Reminiscences of a Workhouse Medical Officer*, 1889)

The type of illness determined whether a

patient was sent to a voluntary hospital or a workhouse, the latter concentrating on the incurably ill, the old and the destitute.

Crimean War nurses

The Crimean War, which broke out in 1854, was the first war to have good newspaper coverage. William Russell's report in *The Times* on the miserable condition of British wounded at the front caused a national outcry. Florence Nightingale, who had already taken an interest in nursing reform, decided to take a party of nurses to the Crimea, selecting mostly nuns from religious orders who had gained their nursing experience in the slums or tending victims of cholera epidemics. The nurses received between 12s. and 14s. a week, plus keep, and a distinctive uniform – a heavy grey dress and jacket, covered by a short cloak, and an unbecoming cap. Although soldiers' wives and camp followers had once done military nursing, by 1854 it was the duty of male orderlies. Initially, Miss Nightingale's nurses were not welcomed by the army, but they soon proved their worth. Two nuns of the Anglican Sellon Order wrote about their experiences. The first, Sarah Anne Terrot, describes her arrival at the Barrack Hospital, Scutari:

Here we found a quantity of straw and sacking made up hastily into beds, and we were desired to sew them up . . . as wounded patients were immediately expected. (Quoted in Robert G. Richardson [ed.], *Nurse Sarah Anne With Florence Nightingale in Scutari*)

The soldiers arrived in a pitiful state, their wounds still untreated from the battle four days earlier. The nurses undressed them and put them to bed.

We had a good supply of warm water, lint, oilskin, and strapping, and each had a basin, so in a short time each patient had not only the comfort of having his stiff and painful wounds dressed, but of a good wash besides . . . . Except cod-liver oil, I very seldom had anything to do with medicine.

Another nurse from the same Order, Margaret Goodman, comments:

Night is specially trying to the sick and wretched, and then on all sides arose the moan of pain or the murmur of delirium. At this period there were no night nurses, but Miss Nightingale, lamp in hand, each night traversed alone the four miles of beds. (Quoted in *A Hundred Years of Medical Care*)

Nightingale Training School

Before the Nightingale Training School opened in 1860, there had been earlier attempts to give training to nurses, particularly within the religious orders. Both Florence Nightingale and Elizabeth Fry had been influenced by the Deaconess nurses trained at the Kaiserswerth Institute in Germany, and King's College Hospital had taken in pupils since 1856. The difference between the Nightingale school and earlier training establishments was that it aimed to raise the skill and status of nursing by providing a professional training which would be recognized by any hospital, making a senior nurse or matron in charge of the nurses, rather than a male administrator. Tuition was both practical and theoretical, and students' work was evaluated under the headings 'Personal Character' and 'Technical Record'. Pupils kept ward diaries which were seen and commented on astringently by Miss Nightingale. Unlucky 'Miss B.' was described: 'As poor a two-fisted thing as ever I saw. No love of the thing. No heart in it. Wants amusement. Has plenty of time in the afternoon for Diaries and Cases but wants to go out and do needlework.' 'Miss H.' was dismissed with: 'If there is anything in her, it requires a hand pump to get it out' (quoted in *A Hundred Years of Medical Care*). Florence Nightingale expected a high moral standard from her nurses. This, and the fact that nurses 'lived in' at a nurses' home under strict discipline, meant that the profession became more respectable, and middle-class parents became less unwilling for their daughters to enrol as Special Probationers.

Rachel Strong, one of the first nurses at the

SISTER   NURSE   LADY PROBATIONER

UNIFORMS AT THE MIDDLESEX HOSPITAL, 1895

6 *Uniforms at the Middlesex Hospital, 1895. The
sister's dress is purple, the nurse wears light mauve
and the lady probationer is in black.*

HOW TO BECOME A NURSE

PRICE
2/-
NET

Edited by
SIR HENRY
BURDETT,
K.C.B., K.C.V.O.

Nightingale Training School, said that there was little actual nursing to do at that time, particularly as the 'taking of temperatures and pulses, and the common tests for urine were strictly speaking medical students' work'. Nurses worked from 8 a.m. to 8 p.m., with two hours off in the afternoon, for seven days a week.

It was exceptional to receive a clean patient, and baths being limited there was much washing in bed . . . . The ward kitchen was also an operating room, the mere mention of which, I think, is sufficient . . . . You can readily understand the terrible results of such an arrangement, no sterilizers, and none of the numerous precautions taken today. (Rachel Strong, *Recollections of Surrey Gardens*, 1867)

Uniform

The style of clothing Florence Nightingale decided would be suitable for nurses was a cross between that worn by nursing nuns and that of a servant in the 1860s. It was common at that time for women to wear lace or linen caps indoors and these soon became identified with a nurse's role. No crinolines were allowed. Miss Nightingale believed it better to 'avoid washing stuffs; they require endless change to look decent.' Many variations of dress and cap developed within the different hospitals and by 1889 even pauper nurses wore a uniform. The matron always dressed differently from her nurses. There is no doubt that their distinctive uniform helped nurses to look professional, and the small differences in belts and caps to show rank gave a feeling of almost military discipline to the profession.

Special Probationers

Training schools on the Nightingale model soon opened in other hospitals over the country. Age of

7   *Cover of a book about careers in nursing at the turn of the century*

entry was usually between 25 and 35, although there were exceptions. This restricted recruitment as many girls had to get jobs immediately they left school. A handbook printed shortly before the Great War advised potential Special Probationers to fill in the time between school and nursing by keeping their brains active, rising early and living a healthy life, suggesting it was:

. . . an excellent plan for a girl to place herself for a few hours every day under the orders of an upper servant and learn systematically to clean out a room, dust, sweep, clean out grates, clean silver, lay the cloth, light fires, etc. (Sir Henry Burdett, *How to Become A Nurse*)

By 1890 salaries for student nurses averaged between £10 and £20 a year, increasing in the early years of this century to £26, but the real value was higher because of free food, lodgings, laundry and uniforms. Head nurses, or sisters, received between £30 and £60. Such salaries compared well with those earned in the factory or in service, but ordinary teachers could get around £50 a year and a Post Office Clerk between £65 and £80, although, of course, they had to pay board, lodgings, laundry and clothes out of this.

One of the first Special Probationers admitted to St Bartholomew's Hospital in 1877 found that the matron 'greatly disapproved of such an innovation as "lady nurses".' She shared a room opening into the ward with a nurse who drank heavily:

It was very usual for the friends to bring in presents of gin to bribe the nurses to be kind to the patients.

The work was very hard:

. . . lockers, locker-boards, and tables, of course, to scrub every day. Luke was the only ward where the floor was scrubbed daily, each nurse doing her half, and Sister herself lending a hand if they were very busy . . . . One thought nothing of having fourteen or fifteen poultices to change. All wounds, of course, suppurated, and required

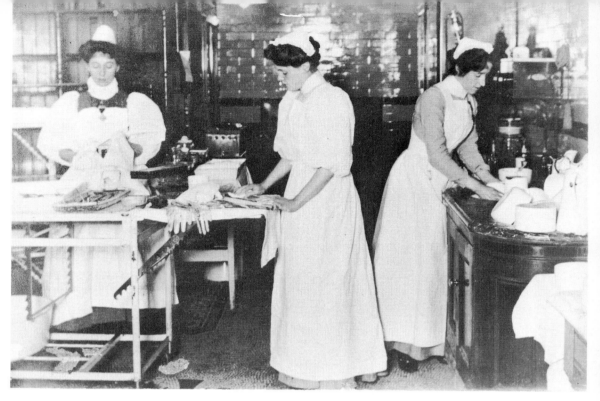

8 *Nurses sterilizing instruments at Charing Cross Hospital in the 1900s*

dressing or poulticing twice or three times a day . . . . The only baths in the wards were in the kitchens, and were covered over with wooden covers, which often served as a table on which to carve the dinners. (*Journal of St Bartholomew's Nurses League,* May 1902)

District nursing

Nursing at home rather than in hospital is the oldest form of nursing care. Florence Nightingale was responsible for starting a training scheme at Liverpool Infirmary in 1861 for 'nurse missioners', the predecessors of district nurses. These nurse missioners were taught to work in the community and, in 1874, the Metropolitan Nursing Association was formed, which provided a two-year training. Queen Victoria, who was always interested in nursing, offered £70,000 for the improvement of district nursing and in 1888 the Queen Victoria Jubilee Institute for Nurses was founded. C.M. Somerville describes the work of a typical district nurse in 1893. Her day started at 8 a.m., when she went to see:

. . . a little girl with bronchial pneumonia and whooping-cough . . . as her temperature is high, I give her a sponge bath, I then rub her chest with camphorated oil, and put on a cotton jacket I had made for her. Then I go to see a little boy just recovering from pneumonia, who is weak and very stiff. I give him a good rubbing, and show his mother how to make a custard and beef-tea for him.

Of her ten cases that day almost all are small children and only one is over 70.

Midwives

Meanwhile, midwives had also been trying to raise the status of their profession. The Victorians were so prudish that even the word 'midwife' was considered not quite respectable. In 1888 an independent midwife charged a Poor Law patient between 4s. and 7s. a visit, whilst 'trades-people' would be charged £1. 1s. Midwives on the staff of a hospital or Poor Law infirmary received between £25 and £30 a year. They were

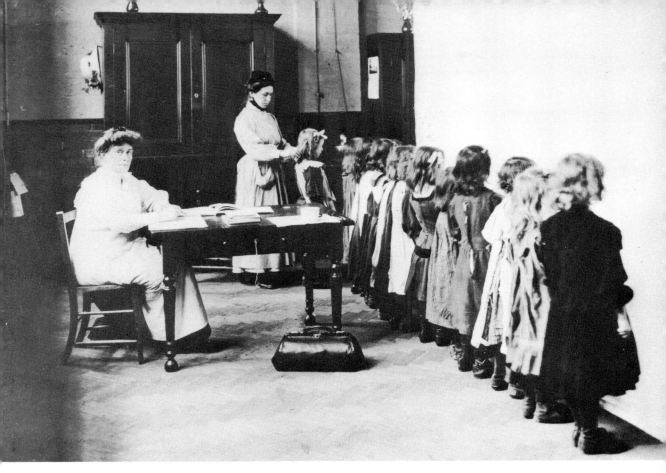

generally married and older than other nurses. In 1902 the Midwives Act was passed, giving the profession state registration of a kind, but forcing midwives to apply to the local authorities for a licence to practice. Without proper means of birth control families were large at the end of the nineteenth century. Most babies were born at home and many died at birth, or within the next few months, and about 2500 mothers also died in childbirth every year due to poor standards of health and housing.

Health visitors

The need for medicine to prevent disease as well as to cure it was first recognized by public health pioneer Edwin Chadwick in the early nineteenth century. In 1848 the Public Health Act was passed and, soon after, the first medical officers of health were appointed. Through various Local Government Acts during the 1880s and 1890s

9 *A school nurse examines children's hair for nits, 1911. She was known to everyone as 'Nitty Nora'.*

these medical officers of health became responsible to local councils. The health visitors who worked for them had, like district nurses, evolved from 'health missioners', who had been sent out by the Ladies' Sanitary Association in Manchester to advise slum dwellers on matters of hygiene and general health. Health visiting was at first seen as a separate profession from nursing, but by the Health Visitors (London) Order of 1902 a medical or nursing training, or a certificate from an 'approved society' became compulsory. The health visitors' role was preventative medicine, not nursing the sick, and their job was to visit mothers in their homes and advise them on the care of their babies and young children. From 1907 they also conducted school medical inspections.

10 A cartoon indicating that there were too many untrained voluntary Red Cross workers during the Boer War and not enough real nurses

Mental nursing

Before the nineteenth century, mental nursing was a grim story. The insane were kept in chains, starved, beaten, purged or put on display for people to jeer at. As treatment and conditions improved a new kind of nurse was needed, but the emphasis remained on restraint rather than therapy until medical knowledge improved after the Second World War.

Opium and morphia were used as sedatives. Male and female patients were separated and cared for by members of their own sex. Women hoping to become mental nurses were warned that the work:

. . . is sometimes dangerous; and the mental nurse must be prepared to perform tasks from which the uninitiated would shrink with disgust. She must not expect that public recognition which her sister in the general hospital receives. (*How to Become a Nurse*)

Men could also become mental nurses, but could only get a general training in the armed forces or at the National Hospital for the Paralysed and Epileptic.

Other kinds of nursing

There were also opportunities for nursing in the army and navy, and there were chances to work abroad in the colonies. The first industrial nurses were being appointed. Some found private nursing more attractive than the strict discipline of a hospital. Specialized training could be obtained at children's hospitals or fever hospitals.

Nursing had come a long way by 1914, but every nurse had widely different experience and training. There was no professional standard or system of state registration. This would come in a few more years.

2 The Great War and the Struggle for Registration

VADs

The Great War made new demands on medical services. British casualties totalled 11 million by the time armistice was signed. Women were needed for jobs of all kinds to release men for the forces. The immediate effect on nursing was that large numbers of barely trained women entered the profession through the Voluntary Aid Detachments (VADs). This organization had been founded shortly before the war and, as it was unpaid, attracted well-born women who were accustomed to working for charity and wanted to help the war effort without going through a long nursing training.

The War Office was grateful for all the nursing help it could get, trained or untrained, but many qualified nurses feared that these amateurs might compete with them for jobs once the war was over, and they increased their demands for a recognized training scheme for all nurses and a state register of those who were qualified. In 1915, in order to encourage recruits, the War Office started paying VADs a salary of £20 to £30 a year if they worked in military hospitals. Florine Irwin was a medical student when war broke out and decided to become a VAD. She was sent to Netley Hospital as a laboratory assistant:

We dealt with tests for diphtheria, typhoid, cerebro-spinal fever, anthrax or anything else that turned up . . . . By 1917 there was not much demand for girls in the lab as RAMC orderlies were coming back from France on home duties after sick leave. We heard that they were very short of nurses in the main part of the hospital,

11   *VAD Florine Irwin at Netley Military Hospital with two wounded soldiers*

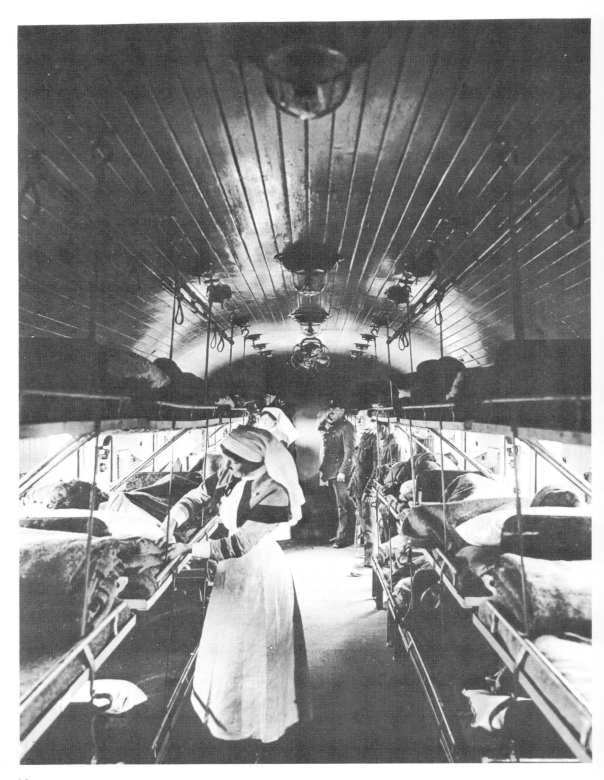

so I arranged for a transfer. I went home on four days' leave and returned to the Nursing Section – I now had officer rank.

Florine Irwin worked from 7 a.m. to 8 p.m. as a nurse, with three hours off, for seven days a week and only one day off a month.

Our patients were a wonderful lot and were most appreciative of anything done for them. One Scottie was a great character. He told me with pride one morning that there had been a new nurse on night duty and he had assured her that he always had to have a glass of brandy each night – and got it too, as she did not enquire if the order was correct!

Some VADs were harshly treated by the trained staff. Their VAD commandant, Dame Katherine Furse, described the case of a new VAD who:

... having done no nursing or hospital work before, was put into a very heavy surgical ward and made to help with terribly bad dressings and even given eye dressings to do herself with no help or instruction from the Sister. She was so upset by the awful sights and the fear of making mistakes that her nerves were upset ...
(Arthur Marwick, *Women At War*).

Mrs Furse felt that 'under the right conditions she would probably have made an admirable nurse'.
Constance Boothroyd, another wartime VAD says: 'The nurses rather turned their noses up at us – we were just nobody.' Vera Brittain wrote indignantly in her diary:

So poor Miss Brittain has so far fallen from her pedestal as not to have sufficient brain to give out thirty clean towels and take thirty dirty ones away! Such is the reputation of a VAD! No wonder I want work in which I can exercise a *little* initiative. (*Chronicle of Youth*)

12   British ambulance train in France 1918

Nursing at the front

Nurses serving overseas often found the line between trained and untrained was not so strictly drawn. Everyone had to adapt to difficult conditions and to improvise, often under bombardment. There were not only the wounds caused by shells and bullets to treat, but also gassed or shell-shocked patients, or those suffering from trench foot and other illnesses brought about by the terrible conditions on the Western front. Many soldiers died of gangrene or blood poisoning. Constance Boothroyd's husband died from an infected wound when he was back in England and staying in Lady Carnarvon's convalescent home. His widow says: 'These days he wouldn't have died, because of penicillin.' Gas patients were difficult to nurse as the smell seemed to cling to them, even after they had been washed and their clothes changed. Many nurses became mildly gassed themselves, with sore eyes, sickness and shortness of breath. Nurses worked in hospitals, casualty clearing stations, hospital barges and ambulance trains. Trains carried about 500 patients, most of them critically ill as they came straight from the front line.

The Queen Alexandra's Imperial Military Nursing Service (QAIMNS) and the naval branch, Queen Alexandra's Royal Naval Nursing Service (QARNNS) had been founded shortly before the war. A nursing reserve had been formed in 1910, for which civilian hospitals agreed to supply nurses if war broke out. One QA reservist, Irene Laying, who had trained at University College Hospital before the war, joined the British 21st General Hospital in Salonika in 1915, which had been run up to that time by RAMC doctors and orderlies. Nursing conditions were very bad.

Until the arrival of the nurses ... at night the tents were securely fastened up by the RAMC orderlies and the patients left without supervision.

There were many cases of malaria, dysentery and pneumonia, and the death rate was high. Another QA nurse, Lady Harkness, who served in France, found the wounds she had to treat:

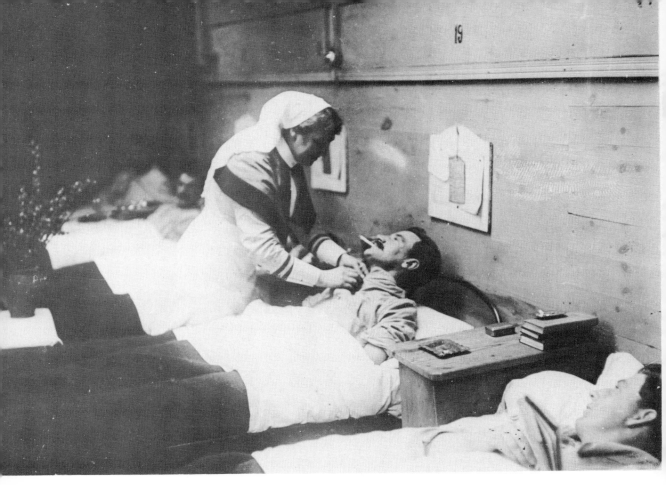

13   *Ward on a hospital barge in France, 1918*

... were in most cases frightful, and had only received first aid in a casualty clearing station. They had been given anti-Tetanus serum, antibiotics were then not known, and if gas gangrene had started there was little hope of saving life.

On the way to her next posting in Egypt in 1917, Lady Harkness's ship was torpedoed, but she survived to work in Cairo, dealing with casualties from the Palestine front, many of whom had dysentery, malaria and bilharzia. 'However, their progress to recovery was rapid, with rest, codliver oil and an iron tonic.'

Most nurses wanted to go on active service as they felt that was where the real nursing was to be done. Olive Dent served in France for two years in a tented hospital with no hot water, taps, sinks, fires or gas stoves and sometimes 'only six wash bowls for the washing of 140 patients'. Night duty started at 7.15 p.m. with:

... a meal of roast beef and boiled turnips .... We each take our lighted lantern as we leave the mess, and trudge down to the many rows of long tents whitely glistening under the streaming light of a brilliant moon. (Olive Dent, *A VAD in France, 1917*)

Every nurse had four marquees to look after, all some distance from each other – one nurse calculated she had walked 16 miles in a night. Duckboards ran between the tents over the mud. Olive writes:

We have made our skirts into a pair of trousers by pinning down the middle, have stuffed the end of these 'garments' into the tops of our gum boots, tied on our sou'westers with a bandage .... In the surgical tents, where

20

dressings have sometimes to be done every four and sometimes every two hours, one develops into a quick-change artiste at shedding and donning garments.

On the Russian front

Florence Farmborough was a governess in Moscow when war broke out in 1914 and trained as a VAD in a Russian hospital. On receiving her diploma after six months, she was sent to the front line in Poland, where she was involved in the Russian retreat of 1915. She soon became expert in treating wounds and working in the operating theatre.

Mechanically my fingers worked: ripping, cleaning, dressing, binding. Now this one was finished, another one begun; my heart seemed empty of emotion, my mind dull . . .

14 *Damage to a Canadian hospital in France, June 1918*

During the retreat, casualties poured in:

. . . the stream of wounded was endless. Those who could walk were sent on immediately without attention; 'The Base hospitals will attend to you,' we told them; 'Go! go! quickly!' The groans and cries of the wounded were pitiful to hear. We dressed their severe wounds where they lay on the open ground.'

The cholera patients . . .

. . . were in dreadful pain; sometimes the cramp would draw them up into hideous contortions and they would writhe and twist in agony. An orderly fanned them constantly to keep the persistent flies away and to cool them, but apart

15 *Florence Farmborough at a tented hospital on the Russian front*

from medicinal drinks and massaging their legs to relax the distorted muscles, we were helpless to assist them.

When Florence Farmborough joined a British hospital in 1917 she felt 'distinctly raw in comparison, knowing that a mere six-months' course as a VAD in a military hospital would, in England, never have been considered sufficient to graduate to a Front Line Red Cross Unit.' She was interested to see that British doctors used 'tiny bags, containing pure salt' which they placed in an open wound, bandaging them tightly into place, whereas the Russians had used peroxide to clean a wound, which was then painted with iodine, before putting on a sterilized dressing.

Civilian hospitals

Meanwhile, at home, civilian hospitals suffered from a shortage of trained nurses and there were fewer beds available for ordinary patients, as wards were reserved for army casualties. Male nurses left mental hospitals to join up, leaving women to take their places. The word 'nurse' could now describe someone with a three-year, two-year or six-months' training, gained at a large or small hospital anywhere in the country, as a general nurse, fever nurse, children's nurse, VAD or someone with a First-Aid certificate.

Some nurses' training did carry on much as it would have done in pre-war days. Edna Smith trained at the Essex County Hospital, Chelmsford, at the beginning of the war. She remembers having to pay for her own uniforms and laundry during training, and also for all breakages – bedpans were her particular downfall.

Nowadays, they just throw them away but then they were all heavy china and had to be scrubbed out. I broke three in my first year and they cost £3 10s. each. On my first week I was on the men's ward – I'd never seen a man in bed before! The first thing I had to do was collect the bottles and I took them carefully one by one. Sister said, 'Nurse, that won't do' and in the end I was carrying a pile balanced right up to my chin. All the men were laughing at me.

Much of her time was spent washing and sterilizing instruments and bowls, and making beds. Visitors could come in only once a week, unless the patient was seriously ill.

Pneumonia really was a dreadful thing in those days. The patient had to be in an oxygen tent and the nurse had to keep putting on hot plasters. There were crises, and after the third the patient either died or got better. It went on for a long time, but nowadays they just give them a pill and they are better in three or four days.

The fight for state registration

Fears of untrained competitors flooding the

Crafty Nurse (to soldier who won't eat his pudding). "COME, NOW—DON'T YOU THINK YOU COULD JUST NIBBLE OFF THAT SALIENT?"
Soldier (pricking up his ears). "OF COURSE, IF YOU PUT IT THAT WAY, NURSE——"   [*Devours the whole plateful.*]

16 Punch *cartoon of a nurse during the Great War*

17 *Edith Cavell (centre), matron of a Belgian Hospital, who was shot as a spy for helping allied soldiers to escape*

18 *Convalescent home for soldiers in Haslemere, Surrey*

profession after the war made qualified nurses fight hard for registration. The College of Nursing was founded in 1916 to further nurses' interests and state registration at last became law in 1919. As a result the General Nursing Council for England and Wales was set up, followed by Councils for Scotland and Northern Ireland, which became responsible for examinations and for keeping the register, which listed general nurses. There were supplementary registers for specialists such as fever nurses, whilst male nurses and mental nurses were also listed separately. In recognition of their wartime service, girls without formal training could also be registered provided they could prove that they had three years' recognized nursing experience. The College of Nursing, which had become the profession's chief spokesman, still tried to bar those who had not completed one year's formal training – which would have excluded most VADs and district nurses. At the eleventh hour the College's proposal was overruled by the Minister of Health and in the last six weeks before the final date 12,000 applied to be put on the register. In future nurses could only become SRNs through an approved school of nursing. A recommended syllabus was drawn up in 1925 and the first state examinations held.

3 Nursing between the Wars

The results of registration

As a result of registration, the typical nurse of the inter-war years was quite different from her pre-war predecessor. When entry to the profession was open, nurses were older and sometimes married, particularly if employed in the community as district nurses or midwives. The typical nurse between the wars was young, single and well-educated. Her life was hard physically and included heavy domestic work. There were many restrictions on her private life as well as in hospital. The age of entry to training schools was between 20 and 21 in 1922 on average, although some hospitals were beginning to accept younger girls. By 1931 the average age was 19.

There were now opportunities for registered nurses to obtain higher qualifications. Diploma courses were started, nursing tutors were specially trained and more nursing publications appeared. A new library opened at the College of Nursing in 1922 and the College arranged conferences for the exchange of ideas between nurses of all nationalities. Preliminary training

19 *Nurses from Queen Mary's Hospital appealing for funds, 1935*

schools opened in many hospitals to take younger girls. Investigations were also carried out into pay and conditions of work. Some fears were expressed that registration might mean that nursing recruits would come only from the higher-income groups. Many local hospitals feared that they would no longer be able to get the kind of girls on whom they had once relied. An article in the *Nursing Times* commented in November 1931:

There is a very definite niche to be filled by the type of girl who is not the high school type at all. She is often employed in cottage hospitals; she is terrified of examinations . . . but does excellent and devoted work under supervision.

Hospital nursing

Although there were more nurses than there had been before the war, there were still not enough.

20 *Constance Wyatt (left background) and other nurses taking crippled children on an outing c. 1921*

Medicine was becoming more complex, so that more people went into hospital rather than being nursed at home by relatives, and more nurses were needed to treat them. Families took out health insurance to pay for treatment. Many of the better-off patients went to nursing homes, which increased in number after the war. Voluntary hospitals began to have more difficulty paying bills because of higher costs, and because charitable contributions were beginning to dry up. There were endless hospital appeals, flag days, garden parties and other fund-raising schemes during the inter-war years, and it was clear that the old system of financing would not be possible for much longer.

Poor Law infirmaries were also short of staff, as pauper nurses were being replaced by skilled staff. Poor Law infirmaries were put under local

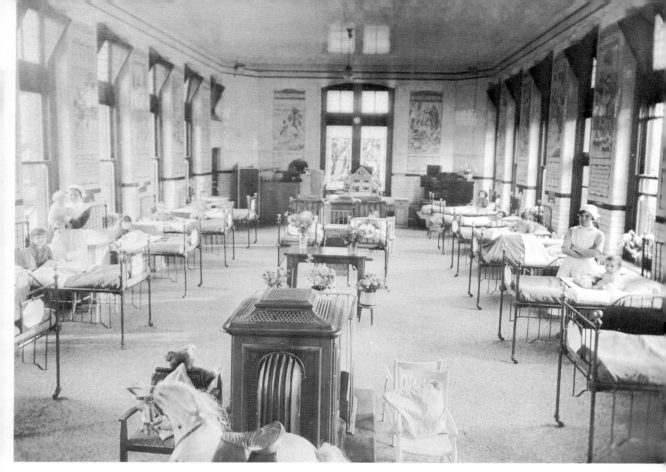

authorities by the Local Government Act of 1928 and became known as municipal hospitals. Pay and working conditions were similar in voluntary and municipal hospitals, although during the 1930s it was sometimes better to work for the local authority, as hours were shorter and the pay slightly better.

Constance Wyatt's nursing career started in 1919 when she was fifteen and a half and employed at a Waifs and Strays Home for Crippled Children.

There were a lot of children in those days who had rickets or tubercular backs and hips . . . . In those days tubercular backs were treated on Carshalton frames. The children lived on them and slept on them. They had to lie flat and never moved. The frames were steel and we wheeled them about. They had little slots underneath were we put the bedpan . . . . Tubercular children were nursed on the balcony – they slept there as well. One winter I was there it was bitterly cold

21 *Constance Wyatt (left) at Paddington Green Hospital for Children in 1931. The walls of the ward are decorated with tiles showing stories from the Bible.*

and I had chilblains right up to my elbows looking after the children on the balconies.

A surgeon from St Thomas's used to come to the Home every Sunday to operate. Constance Wyatt remembers him saying to her:

'Now, if you think you're going to faint, don't faint on the floor here, go outside, because in this work I've got to break the children's legs to put them straight' – these were the rickets cases. He used to break their legs and then put them into plaster. All the plaster bandages in those days were hand made. We had great rolls of canvas which we washed, and then tore up into

27

bandages. Then we frayed the edges and rolled them in plaster.

When Constance Wyatt was 18 she was accepted for training as a children's nurse at Victoria Hospital in Chelsea.

We had breakfast at 7 a.m. and were on duty from 7.30 a.m. until 8 p.m. We had two hours off a day and a half day once a fortnight. We had a fortnight's holiday a year. Our lectures were all taken in our off-duty times at the Brompton Hospital. We had to go in a crocodile with Home Sister in the front, and walk from Chelsea.

The food wasn't very good in those days as the hospitals were all 'voluntary contributions'. I remember that my first supper at the Victoria Hospital was watery shepherd's pie and a maggoty apple . . .

In the wards we had cases of hernias, hare lips and cleft palates, a lot of tuberculosis and also poliomyelitis – then known as infantile paralysis – which wasn't nursed in isolation, but right in the wards. We had no idea that it was catching and I caught it from one of the children – luckily not very severely.

The children were never got up, except just before they were sent home. We never had a day room for them. There was no visiting for mothers or fathers at all, unless children were seriously ill, as visitors used to bring in such a lot of bugs and fleas. We always had to comb the children's heads as soon as they were admitted to see if they had lice, and their clothes were always taken away and washed.

Often children in plasters used to come into Outpatients to have them removed because there were bugs inside. Tonsils used to be removed at the Outpatients' Theatre, and the floor of the resuscitation room was covered with mattresses, where the children were revived by a nurse and then sent straight home.

After three years' training, Constance was made a State Registered Children's Nurse without an examination, as this did not become compulsory until the following year.

After qualifying as a children's nurse,

Constance Wyatt had another four years' training at St Bartholomew's Hospital to become an SRN, making a total of seven years, compared with the combined course of three years and eight months she could take today. Among the treatments she remembers using were leeches, which were placed round the eye for glaucoma.

I hated doing it. We used to have to wash the patient round with milk and then attach the leeches, and when they fell off they were full. Afterwards we put them in salt water and they vomited, so that they could then be used again . . . . Our greatest fear was what the surgeons called 'blue pus' on wounds, which was often fatal. We used fomentations for septic wounds. You cut up boracic lint, wrapped it in a fomentation cloth, put it in a bowl with the ends out, poured boiling water on it, wrung it out, gave it one shake and then slapped it on. It must have been very painful for patients. We had to do that every four hours. A linseed poultice was for inflammation of the lungs. Linseed was mixed with boiling water and spread on lint, which was attached to the chest with a 'many-tailed bandage'. In those days lint was too expensive to buy so we had to tease tow into a square.

There were also pneumonia cases:

You really nursed them every bit of the day and night. You could never leave them. You had to sponge and poultice them – and so often they died.

At St Bartholomew's nurses were paid every three months: £18 in the first year, then £20, £24 and £30 in the fourth year, when, Constance Wyatt remembers:

We thought we were absolute millionaires. One month I had to have a new winter coat, and after I had bought it I only had 6d. left for the next three months. We had our food and clothing and we were always so busy with our lectures we really didn't have very much time to go and spend anything. We didn't wear makeup. We all had to have long hair to be accepted by Barts,

22 *Probationer nurses at Guy's Hospital, 1933, learning how to prepare sick-room diets*

and we had our own hairdresser. We were sometimes given free theatre tickets and we walked to the West End.

District nursing

Before state registration a district nurse had needed only six months' midwifery experience, plus six months 'in district work among the poor'; but now an SRN training was needed before specialist training. In 1928 the district nursing professional body changed its name to the Queen's Institute for District Nursing and 'Queen's Nurse' became an alternative name for practitioners. By this time most of these nurses were being paid for by local authorities. Infectious diseases, dressings for patients who had come out of hospital and mothers with young babies took up most of a district nurse's day. She might also have to attend minor operations such as removing tonsils, which was done by the family doctor on the kitchen table at home. A district nurse, describing her day for the *Nursing Times* in 1923 (8 September), recalls how she was often called out at night after a long day's work:

23 *Christmas time at Great Ormond Street Hospital, 1925*

After a day and night out, the cycling nearly kills me. I have asked for a motor bicycle, but there is not sufficient money to buy one.

Her pay was £125 a year and there were no possibilities of promotion.

Midwives

Between the wars most births took place at home. Blood transfusions, which had begun during the war, were still far from routine. Mary Lindon remembers her mother telling her that a blood transfusion was needed when her brother was born in the 1930s, and a direct transfusion was taken from her father, who lay on the kitchen table beside her mother while it was being done. Although midwives had obtained state registration in 1902, their professional body, the Central Midwives' Board, at first required only three months' training. Many anomalies in the profession ended in 1936 when a salaried local midwife service was established. Mary Baker, who was a midwife in the tenements of Glasgow just before the Second World War, remembers that she was always treated with respect even in the roughest of areas. She often had to improvise with equipment, and many babies were put to sleep in a 'well-padded deep drawer or washing basket'. Midwives wore 'long, grey dresses, white cross-strapped aprons, stiff collars and muslin-frilled cuffs' and, over them, 'blue gaberdines and navy straw bonnets' (*Nursing Times*, 29 August 1984).

Health visitors

Health visitors were also now expected to be SRNs, after which they could study for the Central Midwives' Board Certificate and a Health Visitor's Certificate issued by the Royal Sanitary Institute.

As tuberculosis was common there was a special tuberculosis officer, and one of these TB nurses who worked in a country practice described her work to the *Nursing Times* in 1923.

The first visit is to a discharged soldier who is able to go out, but is under supervision. Enquiry is made regarding cough expectorations, temperature, appetite, time spent out of doors, rest taken etc. Paper handkerchiefs are left. Contacts are enquired after, and ventilation upstairs and down noticed.

Three more patients were seen before lunch and three after. Later 'visits are written up and reports on new patients sent to the tuberculosis officer'. The nurse enjoyed her job, but it was strenuous and she felt isolated.

One big difficulty is to get one good meal a day. Another real difficulty is the drying of coats and boots and the storing of a bicycle.

Pay was between £100 and £300 per year, working an eight-hour day, with no weekend work.

---

24   *Tea-time at St Bartholomew's Hospital in the late 1930s. The nurses' dresses reach nearly to the ground.*

Mental nursing

Mental nurses worked similar hours to their colleagues in general hospitals. Mental nursing had its own section of the Register and a general nurse had to take a further two years' training if he or she wanted to change over. Mental nursing was still almost the only way a man could enter the profession. After the First World War there was a shortage of female recruits and there were attempts to encourage married women to return to the profession. Vicki Hayward, who was sixteen and a half when she started at Bethlem Hospital in the 1930s, having hidden her real age, remembers that there was no contact between male and female nurses at that time. 'Female staff were never allowed to walk with or talk to male staff in the grounds.' Wards were noisy places in the inter-war years, before modern drugs were available to control many kinds of mental illnesses. Treatment was still largely custodial and included harsh sedatives, and, after 1937, insulin 'shock' therapy.

Attitudes to mental illness were changing, however. The Mental Treatment Act of 1930 made it possible for patients to admit themselves for voluntary treatment. Vicki Hayward remembers the wards at Bethlem being well-furnished 'with antiques from Old Bethlem' and there were 'carpets in the lounge and corridors'. Folding doors to each ward opened out onto a

verandah and 'each day we wheeled the beds outside'. Discipline was strict. Vicki Hayward says:

Assistant matron came to me and asked if I plucked my eyebrows, which I did, and I was told they were not suitable on duty. I couldn't fathom how to have plucked eyebrows off duty and natural ones on.

Pay and conditions

The first nurses to join trade unions were the male mental nurses, whose National Asylum Workers' Union had been founded in 1888. During the 1920s the Labour Party attempted to interest female nurses in the movement and issued a draft policy statement in 1926, but trade unionism was attacked by the College of Nursing as contrary to the spirit of the profession. The College did, however, try to pressurize hospital authorities into paying higher salaries for SRNs, as there was no recognized national scale. There were also attempts to reduce the hours of work, and by 1937 the average was around 54 hours a week.

Throughout the inter-war years attempts were made to make the nursing profession more attractive, culminating in the Athlone Committee's recommendations in 1939. It was becoming increasingly clear that many potentially good nurses were being put off by the academic requirements for SRN, whilst many smaller hospitals were still using untrained girls. In 1936 an experiment employing women as nursing assistants or 'orderlies' to look after the chronically sick was started by the Essex County Council. The College of Nursing was gradually coming round to the idea of the 'roll' of assistant nurses, which prepared the way for a new nursing qualification of State Enrolled Nurse in 1943.

25 *A midwife sets out from home in 1938*

26 *Mary Cochrane, Charing Cross Hospital – a typical matron of the pre-war years*

4 War and the Welfare State

Hospital services during the war

The Athlone Committee's proposal for a new assistant nursing grade had not been carried out when war was declared in 1939. A Civil Nursing Reserve had been formed in case of war and this included the trained and the untrained. Professional nurses feared once again that this would undermine the position of those who were qualified. Friction was inevitable, particularly as civil nursing reservists got better rates of pay than other nurses.

Domestic help became hard to get as a result of the war and nurses had to take on more cleaning duties. A Red Cross nurse at the Westminster Hospital in 1941 wrote: 'To be a good Red Cross nurse you must also be a good charwoman.' She found the discipline strict, but thought that most nurses put up with it because, as one of them said to her:

A nurse does get the most wonderful reward. As a shorthand secretary you type lots of letters and wonder what's the good of it. As a nurse you work like the devil, but when you help to save a

---

27 *Red Cross nurses cleaning the floor at the Westminster Hospital, 1941*

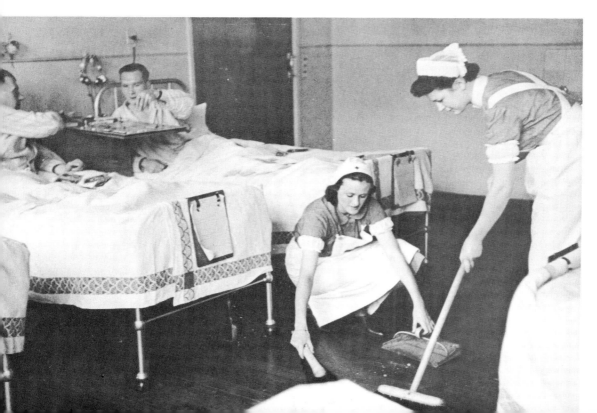

man's life and finally send him back to his family, you get a sense of achievement. (*Picture Post* 2 November 1941)

Regular staff at the Westminster were paid £30 in their first year, rising to £40 in their fourth, plus board and lodging. As a member of the Nursing Reserve, the Red Cross nurse was paid £55, with board and lodgings, plus 10s. towards uniform.

For the duration of war the hospital services of the country were divided into sectors, similar to the later division of the country into regions under the National Health Service. Each sector had a matron and staff based on a teaching hospital. Hospitals in London and other big towns acted as casualty clearing stations, sending out as many patients as they could to rural hospitals in their sectors. Often tuberculosis patients were sent home to clear the wards for possible casualties, and this contributed to an increase in the disease during and after the war. Many hospitals suffered

28 *The London Hospital, badly damaged in an air raid in 1944*

badly in the Blitz, among them St Thomas's Hospital, which lost the Nightingale Home.

Joan Markham, who started her training at the beginning of the war at the Withington Hospital, remembers dreading air raids. When the siren went, nurses were supposed to fill the baths with water in case of fire and to pull all the beds to the centre of the ward to avoid flying glass. At St John's and St Elizabeth's, where Mary Ireland nursed in London, 'all the windows in the wards had sticky paper over them, so that if they were broken the glass would not blow into the wards'. Mary remembers the blackout, rationing and:

. . . shortages of everything. It was also extremely cold. At 18 you're very hungry when you're working long hours and we never had enough to eat. We always had to keep half the beds empty for air raid victims. When you went on for day duty you would find the wards full. Patients were always evacuated to the country the next day, if they could be moved. We didn't have so much blood available to give patients. We used diathermy [an electrical treatment] to suture blood vessels, which was rather a smelly business, but very effective.

Mary Ireland trained in the days before antibiotics.

When we had patients with fevers, we had to get that fever down by cold sponging. If patients were very ill there was no way of resuscitating them like they do now. If they got pneumonia and were not very strong, they died. The only treatment we had for it was camphor injections – you could always smell it on their breath. Otherwise there was very little you could do except concentrated nursing. You were always changing beds and keeping them warm and dry .... Burns were treated with tulle-gras [a soft material] covered with vaseline – you just laid it on, and the vaseline prevented it from sticking. Burns were dressed every four hours, and you hoped that they wouldn't go septic. We used aniline dyes for septic wounds – gentian violet in particular. Gentian violet was wonderful stuff. It used to dry wounds up and sterilize them.

29 *Mary Ireland at St John's & St Elizabeth's Hospital during the war. She used to soap the inside of her collar to stop it rubbing her skin.*

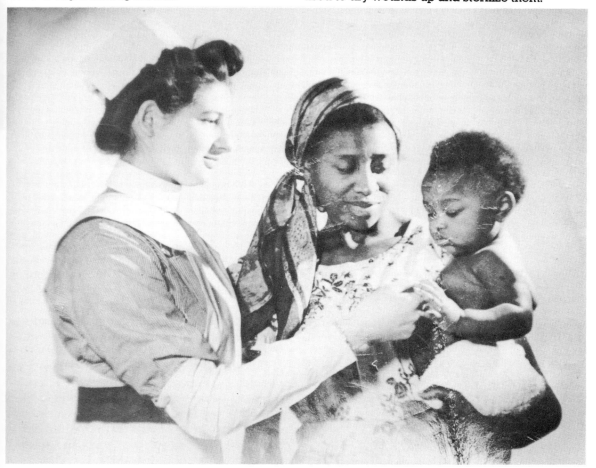

Wars have always hastened medical improvements and by the end of the Second World War many new treatments and drugs had been discovered. There were so many burn cases caused by incendiary bombs and flying accidents, that a new treatment was developed called 'Bunyan's bag' – a transparent bag which enclosed the whole limb, which was then irrigated with a solution containing antiseptic.

By the end of the war M & B was being given to pneumonia patients – Churchill was one of the first patients to benefit from this German discovery, which did away with the old method of tepid sponging. Penicillin was released during the last year Mary Ireland was in training.

---

30 *A district nurse sets off on her rounds in Wales.*

We didn't know what to do with it. We were told that it had to be kept in the fridge but we didn't know whether it was for injection, to be taken by the mouth or locally, so we used to pour it on the wounds.

Trainee nurses worked very long hours at Mary Ireland's hospital.

We worked from 7.30 a.m. until 8 p.m. and we had two hours off duty. If we had a lecture in the morning, then our two hours would include an hour's lecture and an hour for lunch. We had a half day a week, and on Sundays we had four hours off. Our actual pay was £280, but they kept £100 for our keep. During our training we could never have clothed ourselves or had any entertainment without subsidies from our families . . . . In our first year we wore a navy blue dress with navy blue 'sleeves', and white collar, cuffs and apron. In our second year our 'sleeves' were white, and we wore blue belts. In our third year we had striped dresses – it was known as 'getting your stripes'.

Discipline was very strict.

You wouldn't even talk to someone the year above you unless they addressed you. You always stood with your hands behind your back when you were addressed by a sister or staff nurse.

Domestic work took up a lot of a nurse's time – so much, in fact, that a patient once offered Joan Markham a job as a housemaid, not realizing that she was a nurse. Mary Ireland says:

Probationers did all the dirty work in the theatre and the cleaning up. On Saturdays, if there were no emergencies, we all turned to and washed the theatre – ceiling, walls and floor, and we polished every instrument. Needles had to be sharpened, as we didn't throw them away in those days. We sharpened all the instruments on the grindstone and polished them. We also did our own sterilizing, made our own swabs, rolled our own cotton wool balls and filled the drums in

36

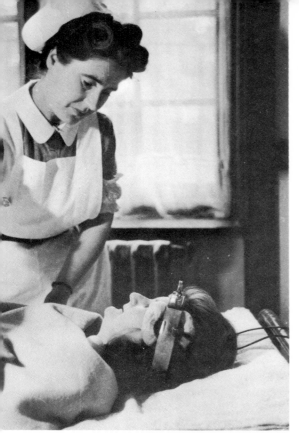

31 *A nurse in a mental hospital watches over a patient receiving electric shock treatment.*

the theatre with towels, gowns and masks. Everything was polished, including the trolley wheels.

Community nursing

Community nurses also had to carry on under wartime conditions. Gwendolyn Askew was a pupil midwife near Manchester, and went out on a case with a 'tin hat and heavy-duty gasmask' as well as her 'little black bag'. She says: 'We were instructed never to sit on upholstered furniture but to take with us a sheet of newspaper.' On one occasion, while waiting with a medical student for the midwife to arrive:

. . . we were soon viciously attacked by bugs. As they proceeded in an orderly direction towards the requisites laid out on the kitchen table for a

home delivery, the kindly medical student dispatched them swiftly with his bare hands.

Joan Markham remembers:

Dressings had to be done with gauze and wool baked in the oven – it often came out a golden brown, but that just proved its sterility.

Instruments and syringes were boiled in a saucepan for five minutes and brown paper was often used to waterproof a bed. Joan was a district nurse and one of her most frequent jobs was to deal with children suffering from worms – sometimes she dealt with a whole street at a time. Before the National Health Service, poor people paid into a Provident Scheme to have a nurse – perhaps a penny a week or 4s. a year.

Nurses in the armed forces

Members of the Queen Alexandra's Military Nursing Service served in every theatre of war from Iceland to the Pacific. During the war the number of nurses serving with the army, navy and air force rose rapidly, and there was no shortage of recruits. Although pay and discipline were much the same as for civilian nurses, on the surface the life seemed more glamorous. Male nurses were also attracted to the forces, and the services had difficulty in absorbing the wide variety of nursing recruits, many of whom were not state registered.

Military nurses have left many accounts of their experiences. One nurse recalls working in the operating theatre in Flanders during 1940 for over 12 hours without stopping:

. . . having one short break of about a quarter of an hour, when we ran out of anaesthetics . . . . Our sterile dressings were soon used up, so we improvised by soaking the uncut rolls of gauze in a Lysol solution and cutting off a length as needed . . . . We had no pause for clearing up during cases; as one man was removed from the operating table another was placed on it. Instruments were hurriedly washed and then flung into a bowl containing pure Lysol . . . . The

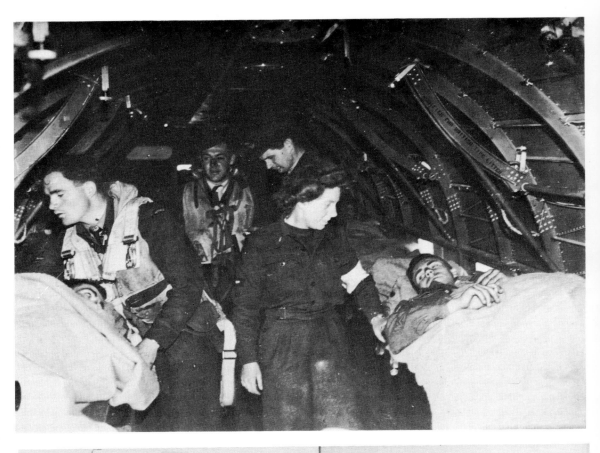

whole day the hamlet was being machine-gunned from the air. (Ian Hay, *One Hundred Years of Army Nursing*)

QA nurses did not accompany the first wave of the Normandy invasion in 1944, but followed close behind. Mary Morris arrived on 19 June. She says:

I was not prepared for the sights that greeted us as we neared Bayeux. The parting of clouds of dust revealed huge tanks on the side of the road, black from burning, dozens of them with the dead crews hanging half in and half out of the turrets. (*Nursing Times*, 6 June 1944)

She was sent to a tented hospital near Caen, and, helped by a German POW, was in charge of 35 men.

Brenda McBryde was in France at the same time at a field dressing station near La Deliverande. The ward tent was entrenched to give some protection from shell fire, and water oozed up under the canvas. Later Brenda worked in a plastic surgery unit for men with facial wounds and at the end of the war nursed victims from a recently liberated concentration camp at Rotenburg. She found many of the ex-prisoners indifferent to their fate, and it was hard to nurse without any response from the patients.

These few accounts are an indication of the different kinds of problems that wartime nurses had to face. Many became specialists in particular kinds of war injuries. Some, like those in the RAF Nursing Service, had to learn to nurse on board an aircraft, or were trained to make parachute jumps to front-line casualty clearing stations. Even the traditional nurses' uniform was exchanged for khaki on active service.

33 *A health visitor visits a family in 1949.*

S·E·A·N

STATE
ENROLLED
ASSISTANT
NURSE

34 *The new grade of State Enrolled Nurse was introduced partly as a result of the war.*

Post-war nursing

Realizing that something would have to be done to encourage recruitment of nurses once the war was over, the Rushcliffe Committee (1943) recommended increases in salaries and a reduction in hours. The Committee proposed a 96-hour fortnight, with one complete day off a week and 28 days' paid leave annually. A pay scale was also suggested for assistant nurses, and this led to the official recognition of the grade later in the year. The war had convinced most professional nurses as well as the Ministry of Health that the assistant nurse grade, which had existed since the early days of the profession, should be given official recognition, status and professional exams. A series of working parties was set up after the war to investigate pay and general working conditions and one of the results was that more married women, male nurses and part-timers were encouraged to join the profession.

The National Health Service

The war had shown that a comprehensive health plan was needed for the country, and in 1948 the National Health Service was formed. Everyone was now entitled to free medical treatment, inside or outside hospital, by paying a compulsory health insurance stamp. Medical services were divided up into three sections. Firstly, all hospitals were placed geographically under 14 regional boards. The long-term result of this was to blur the old distinctions between voluntary, private and municipal hospitals. Non-teaching and less attractive hospitals soon found it difficult to recruit nurses, as in the past they had often offered higher salaries to offset their other

35 *A 'blue baby' (born with an abnormality of the heart) is nursed in an oxygen tent at the Middlesex Hospital, 1950.*

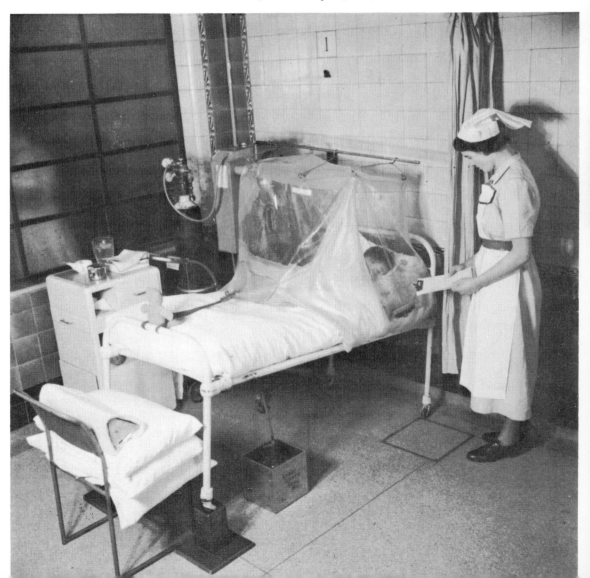

36 *Student nurses learning anatomy. Many overseas students were recruited after the war.*

disadvantages. The second part of the new Health Service dealt with general practitioners, who were now placed under their own local executive councils, and the third part was concerned with community services. All community nurses, such as the district nurse, the health visitor and the midwife, remained under the local authority, together with the medical officer of health. This separation between hospital and community nurses continued for the next 26 years.

One of the first jobs of the new Health Service was to agree national pay scales for its employees. For nurses this meant standard rates of pay and conditions of work, negotiated by means of the new Whitley Councils. The first pay settlement in 1949 gave student nurses salaries of between £200 and £225 a year, a qualified assistant/enrolled nurse between £285 and £385, a staff nurse between £315 and £415 and a ward sister between £375 and £500. The matron of a large hospital had a salary starting at around £800.

Other direct results of nationalization were that equipment and supplies became standardized. Services such as laundry and meals were centralized and these changes would have far-reaching effects on nurses' working lives over the next 15 years.

5 The First 20 Years of the Health Service

Post-war health and medicine

In the post-war period the Welfare State brought improved health and some of the problems caused by bad housing and poor hygiene declined. Infectious diseases were no longer so dangerous because of new vaccines and drugs, and the Register for specialized fever nurses closed in 1966. There were fewer cases of tuberculosis, in part because of the policy of mass radiography commencing in 1943, and also because of the new BCG innoculation. The Clean Air Acts of 1956 and 1968 stopped smog – thick polluted fog, which had been common in London and big cities – and there was a consequent decline in bronchial disease. On the other hand, cancer and heart disease were causing nearly one-third of deaths by 1960. Lung cancer was a particular problem, as people smoked a great deal during and after the war, and there was no propaganda against smoking in the immediate post-war period.

The composition of society was also changing. By 1962, because of improved living conditions and medical treatment, there were more than 6 million people over 65, compared with one and a half million at the beginning of the century. Before the war, the elderly had been cared for by relations, but now many wives went out to work, and some outside nursing care was needed.

Hospital nursing

New techniques in medicine and surgery, for which new nursing skills were needed, had been pioneered during the war and as a result of research carried out for the space programme during the 1950s and 1960s. Hospital management and equipment were becoming standardized. During the first ten years of the Health Service the number of in-patients rose by 25 per cent, although the number of beds increased by only 4 per cent. This was feasible because patients were discharged earlier. Many of the 'housekeeping' tasks once performed by nurses were taken away to leave them free to use their nursing skills, although practice varied very much from hospital to hospital. Generally, most nurses no longer sorted laundry, arranged flowers or did so much cleaning, and a dietician was responsible for special diets. However, those who were nursing in the 1950s remember that scrubbing, sterilizing and bedmaking took up a disproportionate amount of their time. Hospital visiting hours were strict, even in the case of children, and parents could not stay with them as they sometimes can today. At Great Ormond Street in the early 1950s, Mary Lindon was distressed to see how the young children 'screamed and cried, and they adopted the nurses in the end. When mother only came once a week they didn't know who she was after three months.' Conditions improved after the Platt Report on The Welfare of Children in Hospital in 1959, which recommended special units for sick children.

37 *A ward at the Royal Infirmary, Huddersfield 1967, where the atmosphere is much more informal than in the typical Nightingale ward of the 1930s (figure 21)*

Mary Lindon, who nursed at the Middlesex Hospital in the early 1950s, remembers the long hours. On night duty:

. . . we did 7 p.m. to 7 a.m., and you had to give patients breakfast and do all the morning treatments before breakfast. Nowadays they just give them a cup of tea and the day staff come on and do breakfast . . . . It was the duty of the night staff to cut up all the dressings and make all the bandages.

Bandages were cut from a 'sheet of bandage' and sewn together:

. . . you didn't have those marvellous tube dressings then. You always had to bandage legs and arms, and one of the exams you had was to bandage a shoulder. All sterilizing was done at night – masses of sterilizers full of boiling water and tongs – how anything ever remained sterile I can't imagine. Nowadays, with everything in packs, its so different . . . . Certainly sterilizing instruments in theatre was an enormous palaver. You always had boiling going on everywhere, and the place was always filled with steam. Whole trollies were laid out and each surgeon had his own choice of instruments. The night sister would choose the instruments the night

before, put them in the sterilizer and boil them up, and lay them out on the trolley. Woe betide you then, if he asked for something you hadn't got, because you then had to do the whole rigmarole over again while the patient was sitting waiting . . . . Patients used to come back from the theatre with the whole bed under a plastic cover, supplied with oxygen from oxygen cylinders. You didn't just have something over your mouth. Blood transfusions were from glass bottles hung on frames over the bed and the nurse had to count the drips through a glass cylinder and not let air go through. You had a light over every bed with a drip during the night, and you had a chart which you checked every quarter of an hour.

Strict discipline was maintained on the wards. Alaine Clark, who nursed at the Aberdeen Royal Infirmary between 1956 and 1959 says:

One of the things I remember which does not happen today is that awful neatness and tidyness. Before the consultant came round the junior nurses had to go round the ward and tidy it up. All the counterpanes had to be turned down at the same length and all the wheels of the beds had to be facing the same way. Even the drip

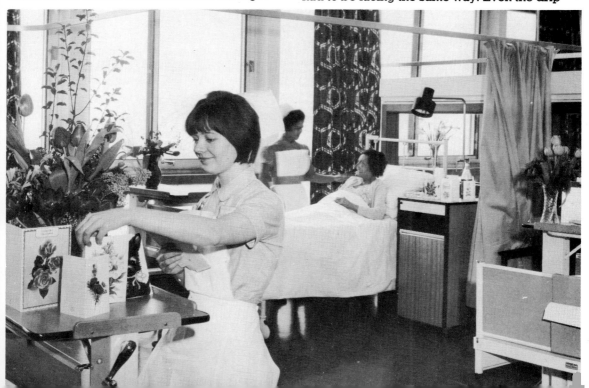

bottles had to be on little towels. Standards were perhaps higher – going into hospitals today you haven't got that same feeling of crispness. Bedmaking was a big thing. Even third-year nurses who were really doing other more skilled things would lend a hand. Patients are out of bed much earlier these days, so there is less bedmaking with patients in them, which of course makes it easier.

Mary Lindon and Alaine Clark worked in open 'Nightingale' wards. Alaine Clark recalls: 'the first one or two beds at the bottom of the ward nearest the door were always kept for really ill patients'. Both of them also remember having to do plenty of domestic work. 'We used to throw down wet tea leaves under the beds to stop the dust rising, and then sweep them all up,' remembers Mary Lindon.

During the 1950s and 1960s most nurses still wore formal uniform, with a stiff collar and cuffs and an elaborate cap. Alaine Clark remembers having a very smart uniform when she started at the Aberdeen Royal in 1956:

About half way through my training some administrator decided it would be much more economical if we just wore white coats with different coloured belts, and they were absolutely hideous – we all looked like little barrels. I gather that the hospital did go back to the old uniform after I left.

No jewellery was allowed, Mary Lindon recalls:

If you were engaged you had to wear your ring on a chain round your neck. I think there were a few married staff, but they were very much in the minority then, and they wore elastoplast round their wedding rings so that they didn't get caught on anything.

Recruitment and training

As there was a constant shortage of hospital nurses, overseas students were recruited, many of them becoming SENs rather than SRNs. Many British nurses took jobs abroad after they were trained. More men were encouraged to join the service, and in 1961 male nurses were admitted to the Royal College of Nursing. In 1964, to attract more nurses, the Platt Committee recommended lowering the age of entry to seventeen and a half. Candidates for registration should have 5 'O' Levels and those wanting enrolment needed a Certificate of Secondary Education or its equivalent. All candidates were eligible for a grant. The Committee recognized a need to make training more stimulating and that suitably qualified nurses should be encouraged to take degrees in related subjects.

One of the reasons for a shortage of staff was that nurses' pay had not kept pace with the rising cost of living. In 1962, after mass meetings of nurses and lobbying of the House of Commons, nurses were awarded a 9 per cent increase. By 1969 student nurses in general hospitals earned between £395 and £480 annually, assistant/enrolled nurses received between £680 and £825, staff nurses from £795 to £925 and ward sisters from £970 to £1,315. The commencing salary for a matron at a large hospital was about £2080.

District nurses

The National Health Service had left community nurses under the local authorities, in the Medical Officer of Health's department. A district nurse's job was also gradually changing. People were living longer and patients were being discharged earlier from hospital. The National Certificate of District Nurse Training was set up in 1955. In 1967 the Queen's Institute ceased to be responsible for training and every local authority ran its own scheme. By the late 1950s district nurses were beginning to be attached to General Practice and became important members of the Primary Care Team, with their colleagues, the GPs, health visitors, midwives and social workers. As a result, district nurses lost some of the personal status they had enjoyed between the wars, particularly in country areas, but there was less professional isolation and the co-operation between the various disciplines helped patient care.

Midwives

Community midwives had fewer home deliveries, as there was a post-war trend towards

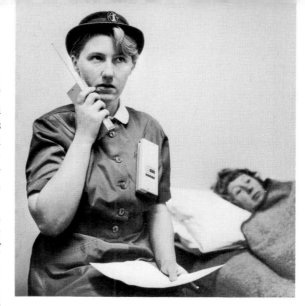

39 *A midwife using a pocket-size two-way radio, issued to Manchester Corporation midwives in 1966, to enable them to call emergency help quickly*

hospital delivery. Hospital midwives worked closely with medical staff, whereas community midwives had called in medical help only if complications occurred. Fewer women now died in childbirth, partly as a result of the antibiotics which were now available to treat puerperal fever. It was most unusual to allow a father to attend the birth of his child in hospital until the 1960s. Mary Lindon's husband was present when her first child was born at the Middlesex Hospital in the late 1950s.

It was a great innovation. I think he was the first father we'd ever had watching a baby being born – it was unheard of – and then it was only because the electricity didn't work and he had to hold the plug in the wall! Now you wouldn't go to a hospital if they didn't let the father come in to watch.

Health visitors

The National Health Service had defined the health visitor's role as 'an all-purpose family visitor', but, in fact, health visitors were concerned largely with the under-fives and with school health. In 1945, under the Child Life Protection Act, they had lost some of their other duties, such as fostering and adoption. In 1962 the Council for the Training of Health Visitors took over as examining body from the Royal Sanitary Association, and candidates had to be SRNs, with obstetric training. Health visiting thus became more medically orientated. Further non-medical aspects of their work were taken away in 1971, as a result of the Seebohm Report, and given to social workers in the newly created Social Services Department. Many health visitors felt that they were losing the essential core of their work, particularly as other factors which had brought them into existence in the nineteenth century, such as the prevention of deaths from infectious diseases and bad hygiene, were now becoming things of the past.

Mental nursing

When the National Health Service reorganized hospitals under regional boards, mental hospitals remained nominally under Boards of Control and there were few changes at first. However, there was a growing awareness of the psychological background to many illnesses and when in 1959 the Mental Health Act dissolved Boards of Control, the move towards less restrictive treatment began. Buildings were improved and some of the prison-like walls were pulled down. Alaine Clark, who worked in a Scottish mental hospital of the old kind in 1959 remembers:

It was one of those old-fashioned asylums. My only other psychiatric experience had been on a ward in a general hospital, which, of course, had a much more modern outlook. We worked 12-hour shifts. We went on in the morning at 7 a.m. and literally did not see a patient until 12 o'clock.

We were starting psychiatric nursing at the bottom of the hierarchy, and the nurses who were running those sort of asylums were really old battle axes – ideas really hadn't changed about mental health. The junior nurses did all the cleaning – you scrubbed the bathroom floor and you had these old-fashioned polishers, weighted blocks which you polished the floor with. The patients got very little attention.

The greater changes in psychiatric nursing came in the late 1950s and early 1960s, after the discovery of new drugs which helped to control some forms of mental illness. The old concept of restraining patients within a hospital could now be reversed, and more people could return to their homes and attend day hospitals or outpatient clinics.

The Salmon Report

The last great landmark in the 1960s was the Salmon Report, which, in December 1965, laid down the structure for nursing management. This was to be crucial for the future development of nursing as a profession.

40   *A health visitor instructs mothers at an ante-natal clinic, 1954.*

6 The Nursing Service Today

Nurses as managers

The 1970s and 1980s have been important years for the nursing profession; years when nurses have questioned and defined their new role in modern medicine. The Salmon Report in 1965 had created a new management structure. 'First line management' consisted of staff nurses, senior enrolled nurses and ward sisters who were responsible for direct patient care. 'Middle

41 *Pat Freeman working at her computer, 1985*

management', composed of nursing officers and senior nursing officers, dealt with planning and the provision of resources for schemes which first line managers would carry out. 'Top management' was intended for policy-making nurses – principal nursing officers and chief nursing officers – which were, in effect, new grades. The name 'matron' disappeared, the nearest equivalent being a director of nursing services (DNS).

There were more changes when the National Health Service was reorganized in 1974. Regional boards became Regional Health Authorities, each with a team of four – doctor, nurse, administrator and finance officer. There was a similar team at Area level. Nursing representatives had an equal voice in these teams and agreement was by 'consensus'. Pat Freeman, a senior nurse manager, says:

Salmon stated quite categorically that the nurse shared an equal position . . . and that due attention should be paid to the views of the nursing service. I think we have gained the power to influence the direction in which the National Health Service should go, how care should be provided and under what conditions it should be provided – so there has been a big jump forward in that respect.

This state of affairs continued until 1982, when the Area level was abolished and Districts (the smallest unit) took on more powers. Then, in 1984, The Griffiths Report suggested that the Health Service should be run by managers, who will take the executive position, rather than by the old 'consensus' team. Although nurses are eligible for these managerial jobs, many fear that they will lose the independent voice they have enjoyed during the past ten years.

Training and education

The Briggs Report in 1979 was another landmark for the profession, recommending improvements in education and research, as too many teachers

and parents still regarded nursing as a career for less able pupils. The Report commented that although enrolment and registration were different qualifications and had different career prospects, 'the actual level of work assigned to some enrolled nurses is often very similar to that assigned to some registered nurses in the staff nurse grade'. Believing that this situation could lead only to confusion and bitterness, Briggs recommended that every nurse should take the same foundation Certificate in Nursing Practice and some could then take further training for registration. It was hoped that student nurses would not have so many menial jobs and that courses would be more intellectually stimulating.

As from January 1986 all student nurses need 5 'O' Levels if they are to be accepted by a training school. A recruiting pamphlet says:

You need to be bright. In three years' training you have to learn not only a complete set of new skills, but what amounts to a new language.

The old SRN is now called a registered general nurse (RGN). Other branches of training are for registered mental nurses (RMN), and registered nurses for the mentally handicapped (RNMH). The grade of enrolled nurse (SEN) will probably be phased out, according to recent recommendations.

After qualifying, there are many kinds of courses, diplomas, degrees and research which can be undertaken. As medicine becomes more complex, so highly technical nursing skills have to be learnt. Nurses in administration need courses in business studies and computing. Pat Freeman says:

The NHS is quite dedicated to training its people. They offer lots of training facilities – nationally and locally. They don't actually demand of you any statutory qualifications to fill a job like mine (senior nurse manager), but they tend to select the people who have put themselves through various management-type courses.

Pat has an impressive number of qualifications in

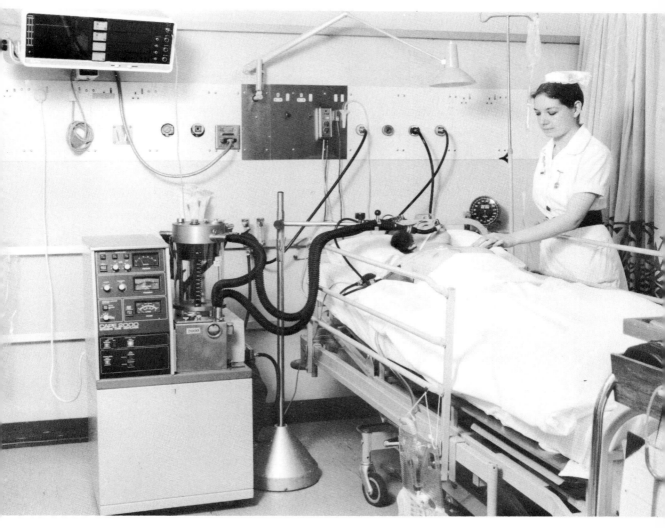

all branches of nursing, including an MA and a Diploma in Management Studies (DMS).

I was always interested in computers and numbers and so when some money was given to us for nurse computerization, I went on various week courses .... The computer handles vast and complex amounts of information very quickly, so we tend to put on it subjects like Nursing Establishment – that's the number of nurses we have and where they are at any one time.

Pat describes her present job as being 'not the

42 *A nurse monitoring Intensive Care machinery*

shop floor, but running the organization to enable the shop floor to work'. In other words, she has to plan the cost-effective use of 'shop floor' nurses, but in contrast to a manager in industry – where the primary motive of workers and management alike is 'to supply goods for profit' – a nurse manager's primary object is 'to deliver care', and to balance the needs of patients and of the nursing profession within the financial constraints imposed by the Health Service.

'The Nursing Process'

The analytical approach to nursing which has been a characteristic of the past ten years, has resulted in a new method of care known as 'The Nursing Process'. This procedure, which can be applied to all branches of nursing, involves a detailed assessment by the nurse of each patient's needs, followed by an itemized plan of nursing care. When the plan has been implemented, it is evaluated and adjusted if necessary. Much paperwork is involved, which has caused some opposition to the scheme, but it can be of great practical value. As Pat Freeman says:

After all, many illnesses are cured by nursing, so it is an attempt for nursing to look at itself and at the way it delivers care and provide a better form of care for the patient.

As nurses see patients every day, they are responsible for their physical and emotional condition. Nurse-planned care sets definite goals for a patient to achieve, like getting out of bed and sitting on a chair without asistance. Mary Holmes, a district nurse, says of the Nursing Process:

In a sense all nurses have been doing is formalizing what would be good nursing practice, and I think it is a mistake to try to turn that entirely into theory – it's just a way of doing nursing well and making it explicit. Having said that, I feel its a good idea and it's the way of the future.

Hospital nursing

In the past, there was a significant number of diseases like typhoid or pneumonia for which doctors could give little treatment, and nursing was all that could be done for the patient. Today, many more people can be effectively treated by antibiotics or high-technology medicine and/or surgery. This is one of the reasons why nurses have been taking a new look at their profession. In today's hospitals more specialization is necessary. Nurses can become experts in

intensive care, dialysis, terminal care – to give three examples. The old days of sterilizing instruments and setting out trolleys are over: most theatre instruments, bandages and dressings come in sterilized packs. Injections can be given from a small ampoule. Even bowls and bedpans are disposable in some hospitals, and much of the drudgery has been taken out of nursing.

Hospitals have become more cheerful places, visiting hours are longer and wards have television sets. Patients leave hospital sooner. They are encouraged to ask questions about their treatment. Ward layout has changed. Instead of the large, open 'Nightingale' ward, new hospitals have a bay system. These are small units of about six beds grouped round a central unit. Mary Holmes says:

I think the present-day layout is nicer socially for people. It's a more human approach. The patients no longer lie in rows. In every way there's a great emphasis on not regimenting people.

Some wards are now mixed and have pleasant day rooms.

The minimum age of entry into nursing is normally 18, but there is no upper age limit. Frances Holliday became a student nurse at 30, but has not found her age any disadvantage.

I'm perhaps a bit more sensitive to discipline and take offence more easily, whereas a younger person would shrug it off, and I do get very tired – but you do get some respect for entering the profession late – people think you must have some guts to do it.

There are still not very many men in general nursing. Stefan Saunders, a recently qualified SEN, hopes to get his registration as soon as he can:

. . . if I do enough courses and make myself look like a worthwhile candidate. I didn't have the 'O' Levels when I left school. The role of the enrolled nurse is supposed to be that of bedside nurse. The administrative side doesn't come into it. But

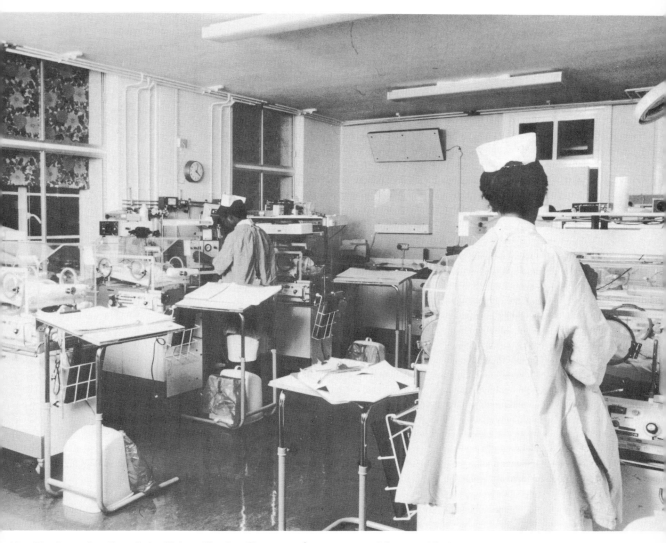

43 *The Intensive Care Baby Unit at Charing Cross Hospital in the 1980s*

nowadays that's all changed – we're left in charge of the wards. Staff nurses and enrolled nurses are on much the same level in most hospitals, even though they haven't done the same training.

A few years ago male students trained on male wards, but now this is changing. Stefan says:

I worked on a female surgical ward, but didn't have any problems with the patients . . . . I remember when I first started my training I could never see myself running a ward, but you slowly work your way up to it.

Stefan wears 'a type of tunic – you know, what dentists wear – it's like that. With it I wear black trousers.' He also has an earring in one ear – which staff and patients accept.

Intensive care

Gillian Williams is a sister in an Intensive Care

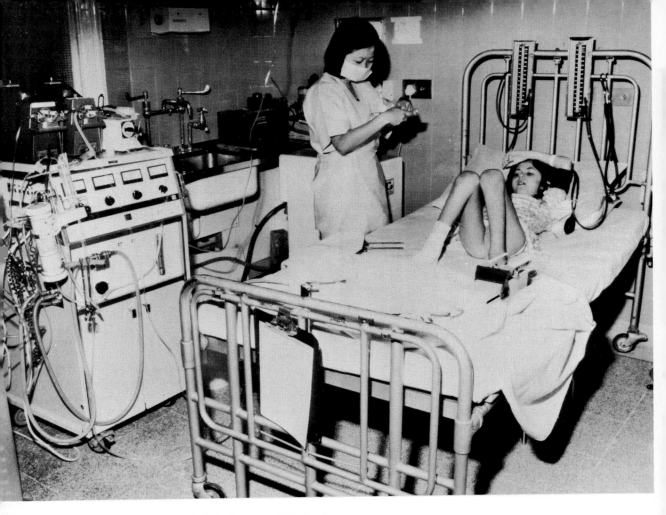

44 *A specialist renal dialysis nurse at St Mary's Hospital with a young patient*

Unit at a big teaching hospital. The number of patients being cared for varies:

That's what makes it so difficult to staff. You can have two or three emergencies in a morning and then none. You try to have a higher ratio of nurses to patients than in a general ward. I think that any Intensive Care Unit is held in a great deal of awe and a lot of people feel very frightened about nursing on such a unit, but in my experience once someone has actually worked there for a few days, they settle down and realize they can cope with the patients and equipment quite expertly. Because patients are often totally helpless, you're having to take over every function for them, and must also know how the special machinery works and monitor it.

One of the most common forms of equipment is the ventilator, which helps the patient to breathe. Then there are the cardiac monitors. With haemo-dialysis you always have to call in a renal nurse, but we would work alongside her and monitor the patient as well. Patients can stay in the unit from a few hours to three months, if not longer, so you get quite attached to some of them.

District nurses

A district nurse today sees different patients from her predecessors. As a key member of the

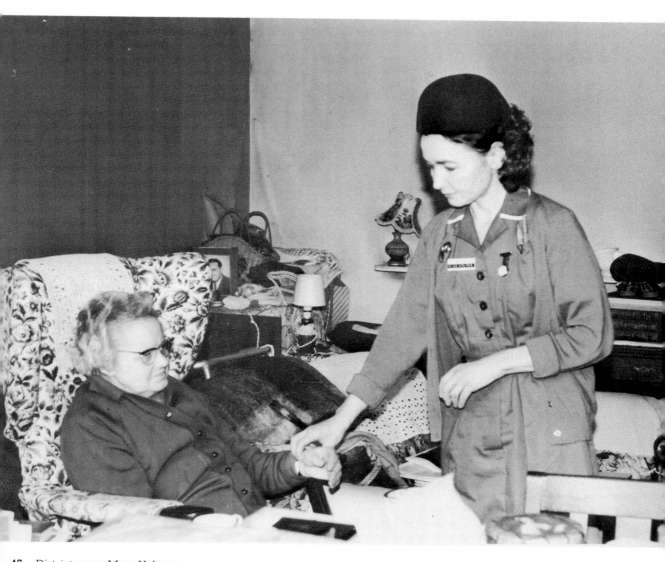

45 *District nurse Mary Holmes*

Primary Health Team she is responsible for carrying on hospital treatments and doing dressings, but a large part of her work is concerned with old people, who cannot manage on their own. Mary Holmes, who works with a group practice in central London, says that many of her patients are

. . . housebound, arthritic, don't see very well and have no relations living near-by. A nurse goes in to help them cope, monitors their tablets

and often helps them just with a wash . . . . Yesterday I saw 20 people, which is the most I've ever seen in a day – my normal day would be about 12. I generally have about three people to whom I have to give pills. One is an old man who is extremely lazy – perfectly able to take his pills, but he simply doesn't. He refuses help with a wash, but occasionally you can take him by surprise. Let's say he averages one wash every fortnight, but you really have to use your persuasive powers.

Midwives

Qualified midwives can work in the community or in hospital, the former mainly working with the family doctor specially trained in obstetrics, the latter with a consultant. Nowadays the two types of midwifery are becoming more integrated. Most births now take place in hospital, attended by the midwife who has followed the case through since early pregnancy. Mothers are discharged earlier and midwives visit them at home for ten days after birth. Pat Freeman says:

The popular idea now is a procedure known as the 'Domino Scheme', where the mother remains under the care of the midwife and sees the consultant only periodically. When labour commences, the mother calls the district midwife, who goes with her to hospital, delivers

46 *A Marie Curie Foundation domiciliary nurse (specializing in the care of cancer patients) attends a patient at home.*

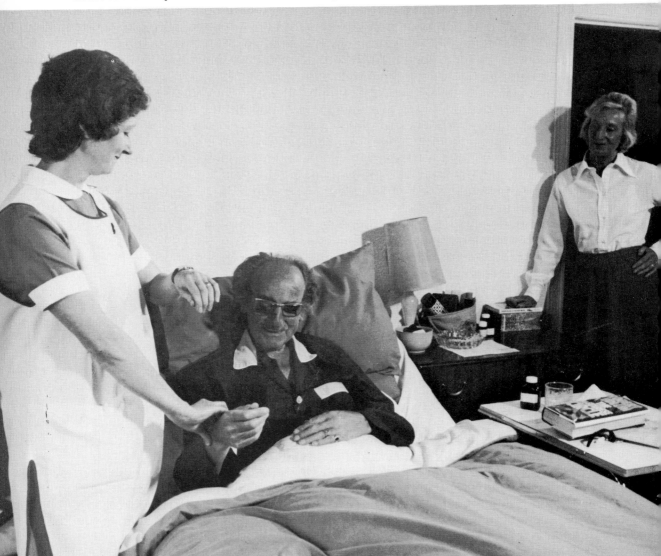

the baby and then takes her and the baby home about six hours afterwards.

47   *A health visitor advises an Asian mother.*

Health visitors

The 1974 National Health reorganization took community services out of local authority control and integrated them with the hospital services. Since Jean Rowe started work as a health visitor in 1972, school nursing has become a separate job, and health visitors have also lost responsibility for the supervision of child-minders, the child care service and day nurseries – all of which went over to the Social Services.

Jean's work today is concerned with pre-school-age children – the under-fives. Her first visit to a family is when the baby is 10 days old, and is followed by a second visit a week later.

Usually on that second visit I talk about things like immunization. I also give information about family planning services and tell the mother about the regular check-ups her child will need.

Her job is health promotion, and among other things she runs:

. . . a little group of Asian mothers who meet at the Health Centre and talk about such problems as feeding, sleeping and crying. We don't do any nursing as such, and sometimes nurses in training find it difficult to understand. Its not a crisis service. The reward you get is a relationship with your client.

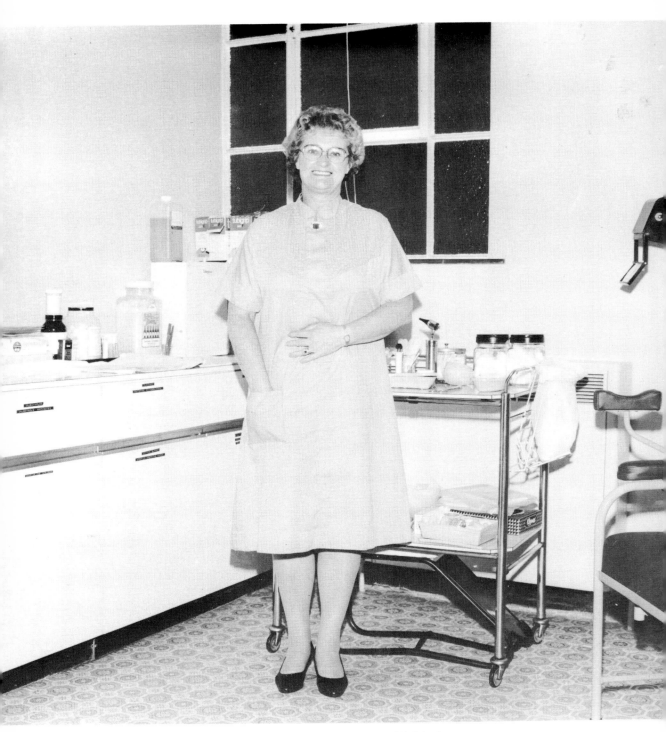

48 *Audrey Gray works in industry as a nurse at ICI (Paints Division).*

School nurses take over responsibility when a child reaches school age, although Jean still visits families where a child is physically handicapped. She also visits the elderly when possible and liaises closely with family doctors in this role.

Psychiatric nursing

In psychiatry the trend towards rehabilitation within the community continues. An important development during the 1970s was the new qualification of community psychiatric nurse. Some CPNs are attached to the Primary Care Team, but so far many remain hospital-based. The District Services Centre at the Maudsley Hospital is an interesting example of the new attitude to mental illness. Staff nurse 'John' (who wishes to remain anonymous) says that the unit has been designed for local longer-term patients.

The idea is that people can come here as day patients. We have group discussion in the morning and then people go to the workshops. We have a ward here in the building and we also have some patients whom we go to see in the community. Once we've taken responsibility for someone as a day patient or community patient, if they then relapse we can bring them in and look after them on the ward upstairs, and this means that the same team of people is looking after them.

Patients at the DSC are divided into three equivalent sections, and 'John's' group has about a dozen resident patients, 30-40 day patients, plus 20-30 who call at the Centre from time to time. Each section is manned by junior medical staff and a consultant.

Nurses do not wear uniform, and this is true for the majority of psychiatric nurses these days. All wards at the Maudsley are now mixed:

There has been a general recognition that you are creating an unnatural environment with a single-sex ward.

Occupational health

Once known as 'industrial nursing', occupational health has become a highly specialized branch of nursing. This was largely a result of legislation during the 1960s and 1970s which made employers realize that they must look after their employees better or risk being taken to court. As a sister at ICI (Paints Division), Audrey Gray works in a department that deals with all aspects of health, hygiene and safety. She says:

Many people think we just sit here giving out aspirin and plasters – that's a very small part of our service. Our role is principally educational – the prevention of a person becoming ill due to the hazards of his or her work.

There must be frequent monitoring of employees who use dangerous substances.

There are, for instance, many chemicals that irritate the skin – dermatitis is an unnecessary affliction and is often caused by lack of care in personal hygiene and not using the protection that we give them. We do monthly hand inspections out on site and at our Research and Development Department. At every opportunity we try to put people on the right road to health. We talk on occupational health and at the moment I'm doing a video on skin care . . . . When I came here about 14 months ago I started site visiting because I wanted to see where people worked and to what hazards they were exposed. We encourage people to come up to ask questions – sometimes it's a problem you can solve on the spot, without the person leaving the production line . . . . We have to keep very full records, because you never know when you might get a case of litigation.

7 The Changing Face of Nursing

The image of a typical nurse in the 1860s was the 'Lady with the Lamp', the 'Ministering Angel', who smoothed her patient's brow and gave medicines under the doctor's orders. Her clothes – part-nun and part-servant – helped to perpetuate the image. A nurse was also a maternal figure, expert in housekeeping and cleaning. There was little change in these concepts until the Second World

49 *Nightingale nurses watching over patients, as seen by a contemporary cartoonist*

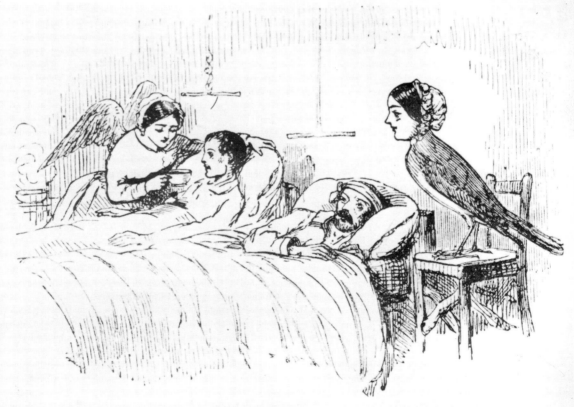

WOUNDED SOLDIERS AND NIGHTINGALES

50 *The Romantic novelist's image of a nurse*

War. Perhaps the strongest alternative image that caught public imagination between the wars was that of the district nurse, with her black bag and bicycle – a friend of the whole community.

In the 1940s and 1950s the media represented nurses as pretty girls in short skirts, who could not really be taken seriously as professionals – the film *Carry On Nurse* is one of the more obvious examples of this treatment. Meanwhile, nurses were described in popular fiction as girls whose highest ambition was to marry a doctor. Today's nurses are worried about their image, and want the public and press to respect their professional skills and reward them financially. Too often in the past their sense of responsibility has held them back from pressing pay claims. There has

been a new militancy over the past ten years.

Even today, a nurse's uniform is very much part of the public image. A questionnaire carried out in 1984 at Cheltenham General and St Paul's Maternity Hospital showed that the majority of nurses preferred the old uniform to the alternative 'national' dress. Typical replies were: 'My uniform is part of the professional image that a nurse should portray' and 'My uniform gives me a sense of pride in my role as a nurse'. (*Nursing Times*, 13 June 1984). In spite of the number of male nurses in positions of authority today, the nursing image is still a female one and only 13 per cent of full-time nurses are men.

Most of those who have become nurses over the years have expressed a sense of vocation, generally founded on practical knowledge of the profession and not on a romantic ideal. Mandy Binyon, interviewed by the *Nursing Times* in 1983 (7 December) says:

You can get a very glamorized view of nursing from the media but because I'd done two years of Saturday morning nursing in hospitals, I knew what I was in for.

Nurses have put up with the discipline and low pay, and those like Mary Lindon who stay the course seem to enjoy their work thoroughly:

I would never have done anything different. I adored every minute of it, but I don't think I've ever been so physically tired.

This tiredness is mentioned by all nurses. Alaine Clark comments:

You make tremendous friends – I had very close friends, many of whom I'm still in touch with.

The 'typical' nurse does not exist except perhaps in a recruiting pamphlet. The nurses interviewed talked about their own jobs, but practice has always varied throughout the country and in every branch of the profession. What they have said shows that nursing today is different in every way from the past, except that it remains essentially a caring profession. The future lies with the new professionalism and specialization. Nurses also know that they are the only people to see a patient every day. The computers and machines which have come into medicine could make treatment more impersonal, but thanks to techniques like the Nursing Process, care can be suited to each individual patient's needs.

Glossary

ampoule small, sealed glass vessel containing materials for injection

asylum institution once used for care of the insane

duckboard narrow path of wooden slats over mud or in a trench

expectorations ejection of phlegm from chest or lungs by coughing and spitting

gangrene rapidly spreading condition caused by the infection of war wounds, in which tissues surrounding the wound die. Today the condition is usually caused by the loss of blood supply to a limb.

gassing poisonous gas was used as a weapon during the 1st World War. It had a permanent effect on the lungs of any survivors.

glaucoma eye disease in which excess fluid presses inside the eyeball, with gradual loss of sight

hernia displacement and protrusion of part of an organ through gap in wall of cavity containing it

incendiary bombs bombs filled with a substance which will catch fire on point of impact

leeches blood-sucking worms once used medicinally for bleeding and for draining excessive fluid in wounds, eyes, etc.

M & B first effective drug for treatment of infections prior to antibiotics such as penicillin

mess place where members of the armed forces take their meals

obstetrics branch of medicine dealing with child-birth

orderlies military hospital attendants

poultice soothing mixture made of bread, kaolin, etc. which is spread on muslin and then applied to the inflamed part

private nursing nursing in the patient's home or private hospital by a nurse who has been employed and paid for privately by the patient or family

puerperal fever fever associated with child-birth

purge old-fashioned word for laxative

RAMC Royal Army Medical Corps

radiography taking of X-Rays by a radiographer. Diagnoses are then made from the X-Rays by a radiologist (a doctor).

requisites things needed

rickets disease once common among children caused by a Vitamin D deficiency. It caused softening of the bones, especially in the spine and legs ('bow-legs').

sedative drug to help a patient sleep

serum clear liquid derived from blood used for healing purposes

shell-shock nervous breakdown caused by exposure to battle conditions

suppurate used in connection with a wound which becomes infected or pus-filled

suture closing of wound by stitching

tow hemp or cord

trench foot disease of the feet caused by standing too long in water-logged trenches

Date List

1854-6	Crimean War – enrolment of female nurses authorized for army hospitals
1860	Opening of the Nightingale School for nurses
1884	Army Nursing Service founded
1902	Midwives Act
1914-18	The Great War
1916	College of Nursing founded (incorporated by Royal Charter in 1928)
1919	Nurses Registration Act
1929	Local Government Act – municipalization of Poor Law infirmaries
1936	Act establishing salaried local midwife service
1939-45	Second World War
1941	Horder Committee on The Social and Economic Conditions of Nurses set up
1943	The Rushcliffe Report recommending higher pay for skilled nurses
1943	The Nurses Act establishing new grade of enrolled assistant nurses
1948	National Health Service Act
1949	The Nurses Act recommending training for General Register and amalgamation of male part of Register
1966	Salmon Report on nursing administration
1968	Seebohm Report results in creation of new Social Services Department (1971)
1972	Briggs Report on nursing education – recommends that nursing should become a research-based profession
1974	National Health Service reconstructed – local authority nurses absorbed into the NHS; nurses have equal voice in management teams
1977	Royal College of Nursing certified as independent trade union
1979	Nurse, Midwives and Health Visitors Act
1981/2	UKCCs working group recommends phasing out of enrolled nurse
1982	National Health Service reconstructed – 192 District Health Authorities take over from Area Health Authorities
1983	SRN renamed registered general nurse
1984	Griffiths Report recommending the appointment of managers, in place of consensus teams

Books for Further Reading

Brian Abel Smith, *A History of the Nursing Profession,* Heinemann, 1960

Monica Baly, *Nursing and Social Change*, Heinemann, 1973

Monica Baly, *Nursing*, B.T. Batsford, 1977

Vera Brittain (ed. Alan Bishop and Terry Smart), *Chronicle of Youth; War Diary 1913-17*, Gollancz, 1981

Alan Delgado, *A Hundred Years of Medical Care*, Longman, 1970

Olive Dent, *A VAD in France*, Grant Richards, 1917
Heinemann, 1977

Elizabeth Ewing, *Women in Uniform*, B.T. Batsford, 1975

Florence Farmborough, *Nurse at the Russian Front*, Constable, 1974

Florence Farmborough, *Russian Album*, Michael Russell, 1979

Cassy Harker, *Call Me Matron*, Heinemann, 1980

Ian Hay, *One Hundred Years of Army Nursing*, Cassell, 1953

Brenda McBryde, *A Nurse's War*, Chatto & Windus, 1979

Joan Markham, *The Lamp Was Dimmed*, Robert Hale, 1975

Joan Markham, *My Little Black Bag*, Robert Hale, 1973

Arthur Marwick, *Women At War*, Fontana Press, 1977

Robert G. Richardson (ed.) *Nurse Sarah Anne with Florence Nightingale in Scutari*, John Murray, 1977

Mary Stocks, *A Hundred Years of District Nursing*, George Allen & Unwin, 1960

Index